LIFE ISN'T BINARY

LIFE ISN'T BINARY

*On Being Both, Beyond,
and In-Between*

*Meg-John Barker and
Alex Iantaffi*

Foreword by CN Lester

Jessica Kingsley *Publishers*
London and Philadelphia

First published in 2019
by Jessica Kingsley Publishers
73 Collier Street
London N1 9BE, UK
and
400 Market Street, Suite 400
Philadelphia, PA 19106, USA

www.jkp.com

Library of Congress Cataloging in Publication Data
A CIP catalog record for this book is available from the Library of Congress

British Library Cataloguing in Publication Data
A CIP catalogue record for this book is available from the British Library

ISBN 978 1 78592 479 8
eISBN 978 1 78450 864 7

Printed and bound in Great Britain

With gratitude to all the ancestors who have lived in between the cracks and at the crossroads, long before us.

Contents

Foreword

One of the most insidious side effects of the authoritarian backlash of the last few years has been the forcing of marginalized people into a defensive position. Hostility towards those of us who challenge society's binaries is common: inescapable in public spaces, at work, at home, at school. Too often that hostility bleeds over into outright violence: the immediate violence of personal attacks, and the cumulative violence of denial, exclusion, and victimization.

In the face of this backlash we're frequently compelled to explain ourselves as oddities and unfortunates: "Why would I choose to be this way if I could avoid it?" "Don't you think I wish I could be different?" With our safety on the line, sometimes this feels like the only way of being heard. Sometimes this is the story we tell others and, repeated over and over again, it can easily become the story we end up telling ourselves.

But there are other ways—and *Life Isn't Binary* demonstrates these insights and techniques in a way both accessible and profound.

Living beyond a binary—of gender, of sexuality, of body and mind—can lead to new sources of both knowledge and happiness. The suffering we experience does not cancel out the wisdom we gain, nor the possibilities for new ways of living. An awareness of the co-existence of these disparate, contrasting elements is at the core of the wisdom we gain. And this wisdom is not limited to one category of identity, or one subset of person, but is something that we can all contribute to, learn from, and share.

Let's be clear: this is no niche issue. While some aspects of non-binary thinking and feeling—non-binary genders, for instance—may seem new, the problem of rigid binary categorization is an old one that affects us all. "Us vs. them" polarization, and the political movements that feed off the hatred this builds, is wrecking damage on a global scale. Tackling binaries isn't an academic exercise, but something that cuts to the heart of who we are, as individuals and as societies. And in this book, Meg-John Barker and Alex Iantaffi face this polarization head on, with both understanding and potential solutions.

Life Isn't Binary practices what it preaches; it isn't strictly a personal account, a self-help book, or an academic resource. Instead, Barker and Iantaffi craft a work that avoids "either/or" in favor of "both/and". The depth of research on display is exemplary, but this is more than just a textbook or a non-fiction guide. Alongside engaging information on vital social issues—intersectionality, race, disability, sexuality, gender—there's an invitation for readers to craft their own journey through exercises, reflections, writing prompts and therapeutic guides. The authors bust myths, ground the hardest concepts in snarky pop culture references, build on community experience and learning, share multiple points of view, and open up about their own lives. A generosity of spirit and lightness of touch runs throughout the book—no matter how heavy the topic, I never felt preached at or talked down to.

I've been living an openly non-binary life for two decades now, in terms of my sexuality, my gender, and my experiences of mental and physical illness and impairment. I blithely assumed that I'd be familiar with most of the topics covered in *Life Isn't Binary*—I was excited and intrigued to be proved wrong. Barker and Iantaffi introduced me to non-binary concepts I'd never heard of before— ecosexuality for one—and repositioned subjects I thought I knew inside and out so that new facets sparkled into view. Throughout the book I felt, by turns, comforted, challenged, fascinated, turned off, turned on. I didn't agree with everything I read—and that in itself is one of the most original aspects of *Life Isn't Binary*. This is a work that acknowledges and celebrates a diversity of experiences, opinions, and forms of knowledge—including the fact that this diversity must inevitably include conflict. The authors encourage us to explore even negative emotions—anger, sadness, disgust—as sources of insight and creativity—an approach that resonated with me in a profound and necessary way. This is not a didactic and exclusionary book, but a welcoming and open-ended one.

It's a common assumption that only non-binary people care about non-binary issues: that queer theory is only for queer people, that only people of color need to talk about racism. Not only is that assumption wrong, but it leaves all the heavy lifting to the people already carrying the heaviest burdens. I was so glad to find a work—this book—which starts with the knowledge that these issues are everybody's business. I'd certainly recommend *Life Isn't Binary* to my non-binary friends—but I'd be even more likely to put it in the hands of those who've never even considered that they might have something to gain from these experiences and ideas. The questions addressed aren't just "might I be trans?" "might I be bisexual?" (although if those are your worries then read on, validation lies ahead)—they're "who am I, in relation to others?" and "how do I make sense of the injustices of the world?" It's about how you want to define yourself (or not)—but also an invitation to think about just how big, deep, and expansive the world can be.

The world is always changing and, right now, the number of people identifying outside of binary categories is one of the biggest and most obvious of those changes. Whether we're at the heart of that movement or watching it with bemusement from the edges, we owe it to ourselves and to each other to learn more. But beyond that, we have a chance to use these issues as prompts to greater understanding and greater possibilities. Barker and Iantaffi have written the book we all need for this moment in time. I'm so grateful that they have.

CN Lester
Author of *Trans Like Me*

Acknowledgements

We are grateful first of all to the traditional custodians of the lands on which we have been raised, on which we currently live and where we have written the book. We are particularly grateful to all the Indigenous elders and people who have helped non-binary identities, experiences and frameworks to survive, thrive, and resist. We are thankful for all non-binary pioneers, known and unknown, as well as for all the people who have written about this topic before us. Our work could not have happened without their work.

MJ: I would love to thank all of the wonderful non-binary people who have supported me, particularly H, Michael, Max, and Arianne for our amazing group, and Rowan for all of the love and learning. Much gratitude to CN Lester, Ben Vincent, Jos Twist, Juno Roche, Sabah Choudrey, Kris Black, Francis Ray White, Kat Gupta, Travis Alabanza, Fox Fisher, Ugla Stefanía, and many more for continuing to be such inspirations in my life and work. Huge thanks to Ed for early conversations about this book, for continuing to encourage me to make it my next project, and for coming up with the awesome title. Thank-you to Alex—as always—for being support, inspiration, and creative collaborator, for welcoming me into your family and for protecting our amazing writing bubbles.

Alex: I would like to thank my fabulous co-author MJ. MJ, without you I may not have found the courage to finally embrace my voice and write what I truly care about. Thank you for being in my life for the past 15 years, showing up with kindness and openness to our friendship, family and writing partnership. I am also grateful to my mom for being part of both my family of origin and my chosen family, and being willing to grow alongside with me. I could not write anything at all without my family, who help me care for our hearth and one another, and without my communities. You all know who you are by now (if not, please read the acknowledgements to *How to Understand Your Gender* as you're likely to be named there)! To Root, who came into my life as I prepared to write this book and who quickly found their way into my heart, thank you for your love, support and for processing all the feelings, all the time. And to my children, Melissa and Will, who challenge me to think beyond binaries in every possible way, every day.

Introduction

Why this book?

In recent years there has been an explosion of interest in sexualities and genders beyond the binaries of straight/gay and male/female. National surveys report that nearly half of young people see themselves on a spectrum of sexuality somewhere between homosexuality and heterosexuality. Further research has found that over a third of people experience themselves as being—to some extent—the "other" gender, "both" genders and/or "neither" gender. In *Life Isn't Binary* we take bisexual and non-binary gender experiences as starting points for an exploration of the whole idea of being between or beyond binaries in several key aspects of our lives.

We've always felt that non-binary perspectives have far more to offer us than just a different way of thinking about our gender and sexual identities. In fact, when we find ourselves stuck thinking that there are only two options, we often invite ourselves—and each other—to think about whether there is indeed a third option (or more). Polarized thinking can often be a response to trauma, and we have found that challenging binaries in all aspects of our lives has opened up possibilities that would have been otherwise hidden. You'll notice in the book that we often ask you to think about what something might open up or close down. Inviting you to consider life from a non-binary perspective is about shifting our framework away from a rigid either/or perspective, towards both/and possibilities, which embrace paradox and uncertainty.

When we turn to the wider world, we see a good deal of binary thinking. Politicians and journalists tend to frame everything as a "debate" between two sides. People divide into "us" and "them" in conflicts at every level from the micro to the macro. Boundaries and borders are drawn between inside and outside. Throughout this book we'll unpack where such binaries come from and how they frequently limit our understanding and our ways of relating to ourselves and each other.

Who are we?

So who are we to be writing a book like this?! While working on it we've often fallen into binary thinking about whether this is a good or bad book, and whether we know enough, or not, to be writing such a book. Of course it's impossible for anybody to know everything of relevance on any topic, and we're well aware that there is a lot of material on the history of non-binary philosophies, for example, or non-binary thinking around the world, that we don't know enough about to do justice to. In some ways this is a fool's errand since even the binary/non-binary is a binary in itself! We explore this later in the book, of course. However, we hope that the range of academic, activist, therapeutic, and spiritual perspectives that we bring together do provide a lot of food for thought.

Alex brings to this book both their own personal and professional identities and histories. They identify as a non-binary trans masculine person, as well as having been involved in bi and queer activism. As an Italian immigrant, first in the UK, and then the US, Alex has also crossed geographical, cultural and social borders in many ways. As a disabled person with invisible disabilities, Alex also brings this perspective to the book: what's it like to present as someone who does not "look" disabled, much of the time, and yet who is impacted by their disability daily. They have also crossed professional borders from academic scholarship to clinical work as a therapist, to teaching, both in academia, activist communities and in Pagan spiritual communities, and most recently to writing for a broader general audience. All these experiences and identities have invited them to embrace both/and perspectives again and again.

Meg-John (MJ) brings to this book their own experience of being queer and non-binary, and a history in bisexual and non-binary gender activism and of researching and reading about these areas in an academic context. This comes together—for MJ—with a long history of engagement with Buddhism, primarily through the writings of Pema Chödrön and Martine and Stephen Batchelor. The ideas of finding a "third way" and embracing uncertainty in Buddhism have always resonated with their non-binary lived experience. Finally, as a therapist, MJ has drawn on existential and humanistic ideas which see the self as plural and always in a state of becoming—a kind of fluidity which is another kind of non-binary thinking.

We'll both talk more about our own non-binary experiences through the book, as well as giving you examples from other people.

Part of our aim with this book is also to be something of a follow-up to our previous book together, *How To Understand Your Gender*. In that book we explored common gender binaries including male/female, man/woman, masculine/feminine, and trans/cis. This book expands on that exploration—in Chapter 2—and applies the same way of thinking to many other areas which can benefit from a non-binary perspective.

Who are you?

We're hoping that this book will be of interest to pretty much anyone and everyone. We're all living in this binary world and all have good reasons for exploring alternative ways of understanding and experiencing. However, we guess the book might be particularly interesting to anybody who is already on a non-binary journey—perhaps in relation to their gender, sexuality, or spirituality—and wants to broaden this out, or think about it more.

Although this book is mainly written for a general audience, we believe that many different kinds of professionals will also benefit from engaging with it, especially if they haven't yet thought much about non-binary experiences. Whether you are a therapist, educator, counselor, youth worker, health professional, coach, parent, or teacher, you might well find that engaging with non-binary perspectives will support your work and practice.

How to read this book

We try to start this book in places that you're likely to be more familiar with non-binary approaches—sexuality and gender—before moving on to topics where these kinds of perspectives are generally less common (relationships, bodies, emotions, and thinking). For this reason it might be worth reading the chapters in order if these are new ideas for you. However, every chapter—and every section of each chapter—does stand alone, so it's also fine to check out the Contents page and dive in with whatever feels most relevant to you at the moment. There's quite a lot to take in in some of the sections so you might well want to read just one section—or even part of one—and take some time to reflect before moving on.

To help you delve into the material, you'll find the following features in each section:

- reflection points: things to reflect on and/or write some notes about, such as your own experience of a particular issue
- thought experiments: invitations to do some kind of activity
- multiple experiences: a summary of the kind of things we've heard several times from different people over the years (not direct quotes, but rather composite vignettes)
- slow down pages: invitations to pause and tune into yourself, or notice how you're responding to what you're reading about, in order to bring in your body as well as your mind (both/and!) and treat yourself kindly.

You can use these features as much or as little as you like. You may decide to read this book alone or with others. We hope these features enhance your reading experience and give you something to discuss if you're exploring this book with others, for example in a book club or a class.

What's in this book?

The first two chapters of the book cover non-binary sexuality and gender in the form of bisexuality and non-binary genders. They also consider additional sexual and gender binaries such as normal/abnormal, sexual/asexual, nature/nurture, cisgender/trans, and even binary/non-binary!

After this, we consider some of the key binaries through which wider society understands relationships (monogamous/non-monogamous and friend/partner) and address some of the issues with such "them-and-us" "insider-vs.-outsider" understandings of relationships.

Turning to bodies, we build on the concept of intersectionality introduced in the initial chapters to consider other experiences which bend, blur, or break binary oppositions, including those of people with immigrant, mixed race, and mixed class identities. Thinking about our experiences across a lifetime we can see that many of our experiences are non-binary because they shift between and beyond binaries over the course of our lives. We then consider binaries such as able/disabled, ill/healthy, and ugly/beautiful that impact so much of our experience.

Towards the end of the book we consider how a non-binary approach might apply to how we feel, and to how we think. We explore emotions and the common binary divisions between rational/emotional, sane/mad, and positive/negative feelings. We consider how such oppositions structure our experiences and explore what a more non-binary way of considering emotional wellbeing might look like.

Finally, in the last chapter, we consider how so much of our thinking operates in either/or binary ways, encouraging us to polarize into right/wrong, good/bad, success/failure, and so on. We revisit the limitations of such thinking, and its involvement in many aspects of human suffering such as conflict and psychological struggles. We offer a range of practices which may help us to think in more non-binary, both/and, or uncertain ways, drawing on Buddhist mindfulness, Pagan ritual, and queer activism, amongst other approaches.

Throughout the book we also draw upon our own lived experiences between and beyond binaries, and the experiences of those within our communities, as well as encouraging you to reflect on your own lives and ways of understanding.

So, without further ado, let's start thinking non-binary...

CHAPTER 1

Sexualities

Sexuality is the area where it's perhaps most acknowledged that something that has been assumed to be binary actually isn't. Even though people often still default to talking about sexual "orientation" in terms of a gay/straight binary, there's at least a common word for non-binary sexuality: bisexuality. And there are many people who identify in this way: more than those who identify as lesbian or gay according to the most recent statistics.

However bisexuality is generally still erased—or invisible—in popular culture, with people who come out about same-gender attraction being immediately labelled "gay" in the media, and few bi fictional characters who don't conform to stereotypes of being evil, tragic, or suspicious because they don't fit the binary. Thankfully we've seen some welcome changes to this recently, which we'll come back to shortly.

In this chapter we explore the continued power of the gay/straight binary in dominant culture, and how it denies both non-binary sexualities and sexual fluidity. We'll also consider how the emphasis on sexual "orientation" obscures many aspects of our sexualities which are at least as important as the genders we are attracted to. Many other problematic binaries maintain this sexual system including the nature/nurture and normal/abnormal binaries.

1.1 Invisible bisexuality

Representations of bisexuality have thankfully been changing over the last few years. In the UK and the US, for example, we have much better bisexual characters on TV in shows like *Brooklyn Nine-Nine*, *Grey's Anatomy*, and *Torchwood*. *Torchwood* still portrays traits often associated with bisexuality in dominant culture, such as the tendency to be promiscuous, overly sexualized and flirtatious. Still, even the character of Captain Jack is much more compassionate than older representations of bisexuality in popular culture.

In music, Janelle Monáe, a contemporary queer and Black icon, used what has been termed "bisexual lighting" in her video for "Make Me Feel": a subtle lighting which has the colors of the bisexual flag—pink, lavender, and blue. Bisexual lighting became a meme on the Internet in 2018 with people showing how it's been used in many movies over the years like *Atomic Blonde*.

The desire for representation and belonging

The bisexual lighting meme indicates, among other things, how thirsty for openly bisexual representation many people are. In some of the memes, in fact, characters that may have been covertly coded as bisexual are included, showing the desire for a more explicit writing of bisexuality into movie and TV canons.

Despite being one of the largest groups in the LGBTQIA+ (lesbian, gay, bisexual, trans, queer, intersex, asexual, and more) rainbow, bisexual people are often invisible in dominant cultural contexts. People's sexualities seem to be deduced on the basis of the relationships they are in. For example, in the past we—your authors—have been assumed to be either straight or gay depending on who we were in a relationship with. This meant that our bisexuality was indeed invisible unless we disclosed it or tried to code it in other ways, such as emphasizing a queer gender presentation when in "opposite gender" relationships.

As humans, we have both a desire—and indeed a neurobiological need—to belong, and to be mirrored. This is something that bi people often don't receive. The impact of this invisibility is clear in the health statistics for LGBTQIA+ populations where bisexual and trans people are consistently shown to have the worst health compared to their lesbian and gay counterparts. This means that bisexual people, including young people, are more likely to both feel suicidal and to attempt suicide, as well as to live with depression and anxiety: common mental health issues amongst many marginalized populations. They are also less likely to seek support or to disclose their sexuality to healthcare providers.

When our existence seems to be impossible in dominant culture it is challenging to imagine being in the world. Even when people are open about their bisexuality, they still encounter marginalization and often bullying in both straight and gay environments. This can lead to feeling a lack of belonging, until they are able to access bisexual or queer communities, and a lack of safety.

Reflection point: Feeling alone vs. knowing we're not the only one

Have you ever experienced thinking that you are the only one to feel a certain way or to want particular things, to have an impulse or to engage in a specific behavior, especially with regards to your sexuality? What was that like for you? If you later found other people who felt the same way, wanted the same things, had similar impulses, or did what

---

you do, how did that feel? Did it change anything in your thoughts and feelings? What difference did it make—or would it make—to know that you were not alone?

Harmful stereotypes of bisexuality

We mentioned earlier that there is indeed better representation of bisexuality in popular media these days, however this doesn't mean that tropes and stereotypes no longer exist. For example, in dominant culture many people still believe that bisexuality is a phase and it is often associated with experimentation and with being young. For example, Brenda Howard, an openly bisexual American Jewish woman, is called the "Mother of Pride" for her work on the Christopher Street Liberation Day March. This commemorated the first anniversary of the Stonewall riots led by trans women of color such as Marsha P. Johnson and Sylvia Rivera. Despite this, bisexual people still do not always feel welcome at Pride events, especially if they are in "opposite gender" relationships. The invisibility of bisexuality, alongside its historical erasure as part of the "Gay Liberation Movement", has led to popular beliefs that are simply incorrect.

For example, many people in lesbian and gay communities still say things like "bi now, gay later" which implies that bisexuality is a phase on the way to identifying as gay or lesbian. This means that bisexuality is often associated with immaturity and not knowing what you want. In addition bi people are often seen as greedy or, as a common stereotype goes, "wanting to have their cake and eat it". There seems to be a dominant belief that it's unreasonable to want something beyond the binary of gay/straight. Bi people are seen as being incapable of choosing, as "fence sitters" or worse, as unwilling to give up "heterosexual privilege".

Alex, for example, recollects being told that they just wanted a "comfortable straight life" when they started an "opposite gender" relationship, despite the fact that they were out to family and friends and at work, and continued to attend LGBTQIA+ events and to be active in the local community. This seemed all the more ironic as the person accusing them of wanting a "straight life" was a lesbian who was not out to her family or at work.

It is, of course, not required for people to be out to anyone about their sexuality unless they are comfortable and consenting to that. Indeed, in some cases it can be emotionally or physically unsafe to be out. However, when it comes to bisexuality, being out seems to become almost irrelevant, especially if someone is in a relationship with a person of the "opposite gender". No matter how open about their sexuality a bi person is, they tend to be read as straight or gay by the world around them on the basis of their relationships, or as not having a sexuality at all if they're single and do not "appear gay". Of course "appearing gay" is often another coded way to indicate not being gender conforming in some way.

Going back to representation in popular culture, the movie *Brokeback Mountain*, for example, is often described as a "gay cowboy movie", when "bi shepherd movie" could be a more accurate description. Oscar Wilde is historically represented as a closeted gay man, despite evidence of his bisexuality and love for his wife. This seems to imply that bisexuality is indeed impossible and that bisexual people are "Gay, Straight, or Lying" as a New York Times article declared in 2005.[1]

In fact, several sex researchers over the past decade have dedicated their efforts to proving whether bisexuality exists or not. These efforts seem pointless and disingenuous when most surveys indicate that bi people are one of the largest groups in the rainbow. We do not set out to prove scientifically whether straight people exist. However, some scientists seem to feel the need to prove that

---

[1] www.nytimes.com/2005/07/05/health/straight-gay-or-lying-bisexuality-revisited.html

bi people do not. This reinforces the idea that bi people cannot be trusted because they might "turn" on you and end up being "straight or gay". Of course people's suspicions that bisexual people will "turn" is confirmed if someone who was previously in a same gender relationship started dating someone of the "opposite gender" after a break-up, or vice versa. Instead of this being seen as a part of bisexual existence, this is viewed as a threat.

The trope of bisexual people as promiscuous and vectors of disease

The harmful stereotype of bisexual people as threats is often expanded to view bisexual women as hypersexual and sexually available, and bisexual men as vectors of disease. The existence of trans and/or non-binary people in this paradigm is non-existent in dominant culture because of other binaries, which we'll get to in Chapter 2.

Bisexual women are often portrayed as "out of control", "greedy" "nymphomaniacs" who cannot be satiated. When coupled with racial stereotypes, this trope becomes particularly harmful for Black bisexual women who are already overly sexualized. This is due to the legacy of Black women being seen as so "hypersexual" that they were "unrapeable" during slavery, legitimizing sexual violence against them. This might lead to Black bisexual women being more reluctant to disclose their sexuality as it often results in harassment and sexual violence.

Bisexual men, on the other hand, are seen as a threat because of their potential to be "vectors of disease", including transmitting HIV. Given that masculinity is already associated with hypersexuality and with men being "always ready for sex", potential "promiscuity" is not viewed necessarily as a problem of character. However the stereotype of "promiscuity" combined with homophobia often results in bisexual men being deemed a "danger" to straight women, because of the perceived increased risk of HIV transmission. The word "perceived" is important here as there's no evidence of bisexual people having higher rates of seroconversion (that is going from an HIV negative to a positive status) when they're in mixed orientation relationships, such as a bisexual man being with a straight woman.

Once again harmful racial stereotyping comes into play here, given that there's a common assumption that men of color are less likely to disclose their sexuality than white men. This leads to the perpetuation of the incredibly harmful, and in fact lethal, stereotype of the Black man as sexually dangerous, particularly to white women.

Where do we go from here?

We realize that this might not be the most cheerful way to start our book! You may be thinking that it's all rather depressing and indeed it is. The gay/straight binary is one of the many binaries in dominant culture that has been personally harmful to us in several ways. It's also one of the binaries that's been recognized for a long time and where there has sadly been little change, despite decades of activism and awareness. The term bisexual is not an unfamiliar term in English, yet what bisexuality actually is seems to remain a "mystery" to both sex researchers and the general public, and to lesbian and gay communities.

We would argue that bisexuality is not at all a mystery when we listen to the experiences of bisexual people. However, when people are challenged to let go of the gay/straight binary—which they need to do to embrace bisexuality—there is often a sense of uncertainty and discomfort, which as humans we frequently mistake for danger and lack of safety.

There are excellent resources about bisexuality which we invite you to check out at the end of this chapter. In the meantime, you may want to take a moment to think about what representations of bisexuality you have come across, if any, and whether they conformed to or diverged from the common tropes and stereo-types we've described in this section. You may also want to start thinking about what words you might use to describe your sexuality. If you are not sure, don't worry, as this is what the next section is all about.

1.2 Non-binary sexualities and sexual fluidity

So to capture the whole of human sexuality we just need to add another "bisexual" box to the gay/straight boxes on the form right? Wrong. For a start all that would capture is sexual identity: the labels we use to describe ourselves. These words may not capture either our sexual behavior—what we actually do sexually—or our sexual attraction—who we're erotically interested in.

Figure 1.1: Sexual identity, behavior, and attraction

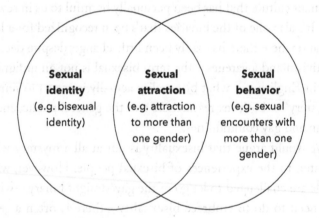

Identity, behavior, and attraction

This diagram (Figure 1.1) demonstrates the problem. If we try to estimate the number of bisexual people that there are, for example, we get very different answers when we study the proportion of people who *identify* as bisexual, compared to when we study the proportion who've had sexual *encounters* with more than one gender, compared to when we study the proportion who have ever had sexual *attractions* to more than one gender.

The overlaps on this diagram are because some people identify as a sexuality without having acted on it (e.g. young people and celibate people), and some people sometimes behave in ways that don't match their sexual attraction (e.g. some actors, some sex workers, some people learning about their sexuality, and more).

Reflection point: Your identity, behavior, and attractions
Take a moment to think about the words you came up with earlier that you use—if any—to identify your sexuality. What assumptions might people make, on hearing those words, about your sexual behavior and your sexual attractions? Would these be accurate?

The sexuality spectrum

Another problem with the "three box" model of sexuality (gay, straight, bisexual) is how we figure out who counts in each box. People often assume that you only "count" as bisexual if you're into men and women exactly the same amount, meaning for instance that a true bisexual on Tinder would be swiping right on equal numbers of women and men.

That leaves us with a problem of how to categorize people who are mostly into one gender or another. If we're defining bisexuality in the way preferred by bi people—attraction to more than one gender—then those folks definitely count. But perhaps we want a way to distinguish between them and "50/50" bi people. That's where Alfred Kinsey's famous scale of sexuality came in. It looks something like this:

Figure 1.2: Kinsey's scale of sexual attraction

0	1	2	3	4	5	6
Exclusively heterosexual	Predominately heterosexual, incidentally homosexual	Predominately heterosexual, more than incidentally homosexual	Equally heterosexual and homosexual	Predominantly homosexual, more than incidentally heterosexual	Predominantly homosexual, incidentally heterosexual	Exclusively homosexual

Actually the original Kinsey research focused on behavior rather than attraction, but these days it's usually used to capture who people are attracted to, rather than who they've actually had sexual encounters with. Kinsey also had an "X" point off the scale for asexual people who don't experience sexual attraction. Don't worry; we'll come back to that shortly.

> ### Thought experiment: Kinseyfy yourself
> Where would you put yourself on the Kinsey scale? Do you think this captures more or less about your sexuality than the identity term/s you came up with earlier? Do you see any problems with this way of measuring a person's sexuality?

The most recent national surveys using this kind of spectrum model have found that nearly half of young people see themselves as somewhere between homosexuality and heterosexuality, compared to around 2 to 3 percent who actually identify as bisexual. The difference between identity and attraction could very well be the difference between a small *minority* and a *majority*. The implications of this are pretty huge.

The spectrum is not enough

But wait! As you might've already noticed, this kind of spectrum is still pretty limited in capturing our sexualities. For a start it suggests that as our attraction to the "same gender" decreases, our attraction to the "opposite gender" increases and vice versa.

We might make an analogy with our taste for hot beverages. We could create a Kinsey-style scale from tea to coffee, with people who prefer tea at one end, coffee at the other, and people who like both in the middle. But of course liking tea more doesn't necessarily make us like coffee less. Where do we put people who really *love* their morning coffee and their afternoon tea? What about people who are pretty "meh" on both drinks. In fact what about people who'd prefer a cup of hot chocolate? Don't worry we're coming to this in the next section and the next chapter... Another problem with this model is that it assumes that one spectrum is enough to measure our sexuality, but we've already seen that we might be in different places in terms of how we identify ourselves to others, our sexual attraction, and our actual sexual behavior, for example.

The bi researcher Fritz Klein pointed out that we might be in different places in relation to a number of other components of our sexuality too. He came up with this list of elements of our sexuality, which we could locate on a Kinsey-style scale:

- sexual attraction: who turns you on (from 1 = "other gender only" to 7 = "same gender only")
- sexual behavior: who you have sex with (from 1 = "other gender only" to 7 = "same gender only")
- sexual fantasies: who you have sexual fantasies about (from 1 = "other gender only" to 7 = "same gender only")
- emotional preference: who you have strong emotional bonds with (from 1 = "other gender only" to 7 = "same gender only")

- social preference: who you like to spend your leisure time with (from 1 = "other gender only" to 7 = "same gender only")
- lifestyle: the sexual identity of the people you spend time with (from 1 = "heterosexual only" through 4 = "bisexual only" to 7 = "homosexual only")
- sexual identity: how you self identify (from 1 = "heterosexual only" through 4 = "bisexual only" to 7 = "homosexual only")
- political identity: who you identify with (from 1 = "heterosexual only" through 4 = "bisexual only" to 7 = "homosexual only").

Sexual fluidity

Fritz Klein took it a stage further. Not only did he suggest that we could map our sexuality—in terms of which gender we were attracted to—on all of these different elements, often finding ourselves in different places on different ones, he also pointed out that where we were located on each different element could change over time...

> *Thought experiment: Kleinify yourself*
> *Have a go at rating yourself on each of Klein's elements. Once you've done it for your current self, try doing it again for your past self ten years ago, and again for how you expect you'll respond ten years from now. Did you notice shifts or changes in any of the elements over time?*

Klein's ideas have been taken up in recent years by researchers studying "sexual fluidity": this is the idea that our sexuality—on any or all of these elements—can shift and change over time.

One of the key researchers in this area is Lisa Diamond, who wrote the book *Sexual Fluidity*. She studied a hundred women who had some same-gender attraction. Lisa found that around two thirds of the women changed their sexual identity at least once over a decade. This happened in all of the different directions (lesbian to bisexual, bisexual to heterosexual, unlabelled to gay, etc.).

She found that women's identities often matched the gender of their current sexual or romantic partners, suggesting that we can adapt our sexual and romantic attraction to a specific person rather than to an overall gender category.

Turning to men, Jane Ward published a book based on her research called *Not Gay: Sex between Straight White Men.* She found that it was also pretty common for white guys who identify as heterosexual to have sexual encounters of various kinds with other men, including hooking up via apps and personal ads, masturbating with other guys in public toilets, and engaging in hazing rituals in university fraternities and the military, for example grabbing each other's penises or fingering each other's anuses.

Jane's work suggests that our sexual identities, behaviors, and attractions can mesh—or not—in all kinds of complex ways. They can all change over time and across different situations, such as whether or not we're in a relationship, in a gender-segregated environment, or in a more or less permissive community.

In his book *Go the Way Your Blood Beats*, Michael Amherst links bisexual erasure to the cultural tendency to deny sexual fluidity. He points to the resistance—and even attacks—that scholars like Klein, Diamond, and Ward have received from straight- and gay-identified people alike. It seems that, along with the idea that sexuality is binary, we're stuck on the idea that it must be fixed in one way for life. Bisexuality is treated with suspicion because it challenges the sexual binary, and also because it prevents us from being able to simply read a once-and-for-all sexual identity label off a person's current partner or sexual behavior.

Labels or no labels?

Michael Amherst points to writers like James Baldwin and Maggie Nelson who have refused to be pinned down to sexual identity labels: gay, straight, or bisexual. Baldwin said: "I loved a few people and they loved me. It had nothing to do with these labels.

Of course, the world has all kinds of words for us. But that is the world's problem."[2] And Nelson:

> There are people out there who get annoyed at the story that Djuna Barnes, rather than identify as a lesbian, preferred to say that she "just loved Thelma". Gertrude Stein reputedly made similar claims, albeit not in those exact terms, about Alice. I get why it's politically maddening, but I've also always thought it a little romantic—the romance of letting an individual experience of desire take precedence over a categorical one.[3]

Let's hear from a few other people who do find labels useful about the ones they use and why...

Multiple experiences: Sexual identity terms

- "I'm bisexual. For me it means that gender can be a feature of what I find attractive in another person, but no more important than something like the color of their eyes or hair."
- "I'm bisexual too, but gender is definitely important to me. I'm particularly attracted to femme women, androgynous people, and stocky guys. I could maybe go for omnisexual as a label as well."
- "I like heteroflexible—it seems more accurate. Or maybe we should reclaim the word 'bi-curious'. Why is that seen as a negative thing? It's where I'm at."
- "I prefer the word pansexual because it gets at my sense that gender really is irrelevant to who I find attractive: it's about the person."

---

2 James Baldwin interviewed by Richard Goldstein, The Village Voice, 26 June 1984.
3 Nelson, M. (2015) *The Argonauts*. London: Melville House UK, p.9.

- "I'd rather use bi than bisexual because it includes my romantic attractions as well as my sexual ones, and it's more inclusive of asexual people."
- "Most of the time I use the word lesbian to talk about my sexuality, because people know that word, however I really identify as a dyke. I like the power of taking back a word that has been used as an insult. I also like that dyke is about how I walk in the world, in a gender defiant sort of way."
- "Queer is the word for me. It questions this whole problematic idea of identifying people by one small feature of their sexuality."
- "I like queer but more because it seems to encompass the way my sexuality can shift over time between different non-heterosexual sexualities."
- "And I prefer queer because although I'm a man who is only attracted to women, it captures the fact that my sexuality is nothing like standard straight masculinity, because I'm sexually submissive."
- "People would call me gay, but that doesn't give enough detail given that I'm exclusively attracted to cuddly bear types with a gentle kind of masculinity."

We'll get into some of the further dimensions of sexuality that these last two quotes hint at in the next section, meanwhile a final reflection...

Reflection point: Back to words
Having got to this point, which words do you feel are a good, and not good, fit for capturing something of your sexuality? How would you explain why you prefer those terms (not that you should have to!)?

Slow down!

You may feel that was already rather a lot to read... Or you may feel like it was just stuff you knew already! Either way, it might be a good time to take a little break from reading.

For this first slow down page, we would like to invite you to get comfortable for a moment. You may sit or stand as you are able or feel like. The same goes for whether you do this barefoot or with shoes on. This activity lasts a couple of minutes.

If you can, place your feet on the ground and focus your attention on the contact between your feet and the ground. Alternatively you may want to focus on sitting down and feeling the contact between your butt and the seat/ground beneath you, or even placing your hands on a steady surface, such as a table, and focusing on the contact between your hands and the surface underneath.

As you breathe, really focus on the contact between you and the support underneath you. You may want to wiggle if you can, or move around, until you can find a place of contact, support, centre, and stillness. When you have found this, take a few breaths there. If you can't find this place, it's okay. You can either try again later, or maybe you have your own way to access this feeling of contact and support between you and the world.

What do you notice from this place of contact and support? What are the sensations or emotions here? Are they comfortable, uncomfortable, or neutral? If they are uncomfortable, take a moment to shift your body in a position where you are more comfortable, or focus on something around you that feels soothing or neutral.

Then take another breath—or two—and carry on reading!

1.3 Sexuality beyond (binary) gender of attraction

We've already mentioned why sexual "orientation" takes more than three boxes—gay, straight, bisexual—to be described. In this section we explore the idea that sexuality is an even larger landscape than just who we're attracted to in relation to gender. Of course gender in itself is also not a binary. Spoiler alert: we'll come to this in the next chapter.

What other dimensions of sexuality might there be? Here we discuss sexual roles we might play, or whether we're engaging sexually by ourselves, with another person, with multiple people, or with the natural world around us. We also talk about the "quantity" of sexual feelings we might or might not feel at all, and which other human characteristics we find attractive or not.

You may already have noticed that we're now talking of sex and sexuality as a landscape rather than a continuum. We believe that this metaphor opens up more possibilities to explore all dimensions of sexuality. Of course, we're likely to miss something that might be important to you here. If that happens, feel free to let us know! We're trying to be comprehensive but, given how broad the landscape is, we're bound to miss some territories that might be less familiar or even unexplored for us.

New models of sexualities
On these dimensions of sexuality Eve Kosofsky Sedgwick, a North American queer scholar, famously said:

> It is a rather amazing fact that, of the very many dimensions along which the genital activity of one person can be differentiated from that of another (dimensions that include preference for certain acts, certain zones or sensations, certain physical types, a certain frequency, certain symbolic investments, certain relations of age or power, a certain species, a certain number of participants, and so on)

precisely one, the gender of the object choice, emerged from the turn of the century, and has remained, as *the* dimension denoted by the now ubiquitous category of "sexual orientation".[4]

More recently Sari Van Anders, a Canadian feminist scientist, proposed a new theory of sexuality called Sexual Configurations Theory. One of her intentions was to formulate a more comprehensive theory of sexuality which better reflected the full range of human experiences. She was also interested in decentering gender as central to our understanding of sexuality, given that the landscape, as we noted, is so much more vast than this. We were privileged to work with Sari and illustrator, Julia Scheele, to create a zine that explains this theory in more depth and we list this in the Further Resources at the end of this chapter.

Sari's new theory and the field of queer studies draw attention to just exactly how varied the dimensions of our sexualities are, and how opening up space for multiplicity, fluidity and openness is essential. For example, how do we engage with our sexuality, if at all, when we're by ourselves versus when we're with other people? Are all humans supposed to have sexual feelings towards others? And what happens if we mainly express our sexuality through a sensual relationship with nature?

Solo and partnered sexualities

Solo sexuality is when we engage erotically with ourselves. This can be masturbation but it can also include any sensual experiences we have alone. For example, we might find cooking a beautiful and delicious meal to be part of a sensual experience, especially if we also enjoy eating it, savoring all the flavors, smells and

---

4   Sedgwick, E.K. (1990) *Epistemology of the Closet*. Upper Saddle River, NJ: Prentice Hall, p.8.

textured sensations. Some people find dancing, in many forms, as well as singing or playing music, to be sensual and/or nurturing experiences, which can deepen our relationship with ourselves.

Many devotees of various religions, across time and space, have also written about their experiences of communing with spirit or divinity through things like prayers, adoration, movement, and meditation, as well as altered states of consciousness achieved through a range of means, such as use of plants, heat, or sensory deprivation. Accounts of these experiences often have both nurturing and erotic connotations, as the person has a deepening, intense and usually embodied sense of their relationship with spirit or divinity. Many people experience this through their relationship with nature and we'll discuss this soon.

Of course whether this would be a form of solo or partnered sexuality depends on someone's belief system. Partnered sexuality is when we engage sexually with other people. Partnered sexuality might involve just one other person or several people. If it involves several partners this involves engaging with a number of individuals separately over time, with several people at once, or a combination of the two. Monogamies, non-monogamies, dating, and erotic play with others are forms of partnered sexualities. More on these in Chapter 3.

We might engage with ourselves and/or with others in a range of ways. For example, our exchanges with ourselves or others might focus on nurturance or on more erotic aspects. Going back to the example of cooking ourselves a delicious meal, for some people this might be a form of nurturance, of meeting their needs, and for others an erotic experience focused on touching, smelling, and tasting ingredients, sensing textures and noticing what happens when food is swallowed and savored.

Erotic aspects are generally connected to pleasure including feelings of arousal, getting excited, experiencing desire and lust, as well as orgasm. Nurturance is generally connected to feelings of love, closeness, and intimacy. Any activity might be more erotic or more nurturing. Activities can also be both erotic and nurturing, and they can be experienced as physiological or psychological, or both. For instance, anticipating someone's touch or a good meal, fantasizing or getting ready for a religious ritual, are more psychological examples.

Asexualities

What happens though when we don't experience eroticism at all? What if we have no feelings of arousal, excitement, desire or lust, whether by ourselves or with others? Many people indeed experience this and often use the umbrella term asexual. Asexualities can take many forms. For example, some people enjoy masturbating but have no desire to engage sexually with others, some don't. Some asexual people have sex with their partners, and some don't. There are many ways of being asexual and no one way is right or wrong.

Asexuality is different from celibacy or sexual abstinence as these are behaviors whereas asexuality is a sexual identity. Ace is a short term that people often use to indicate their asexuality. In the past, sex researchers and therapists saw asexuality as an anomaly and a "problem". However, researchers such as Lori Brotto have clearly demonstrated that this is not the case and that asexuality is just another part of the landscape of human sexualities. This is, of course, something that people in asexual communities have been clear about for a long time!

Some people might be sexually attracted to other people but experience few, if any, romantic feelings. These people often identify as aromantic, or aro for short. Aromantic people might also be asexual but the two are not the same thing. This means that there might be romantic asexuals, as well as sexual aromantics.

Reflection point: New models of sexualities

What do you think of the idea that there are many domains of sexuality, besides the gender of the people we're attracted to? What do you think about the idea that gender might not even be that relevant for many people when it comes to their sexual lives? Do you prefer to engage sexually by yourself or with others? Are there both erotic and nurturance domains of sexuality in your life and, if so, what are they? Do you experience sexual or romantic feelings? If so, how do you experience and express them? If not, how do people in your life respond to this?

Ecosexuality

Many people experience a deep sensual, erotic connection to the earth. For example, some have deeply erotic experiences with water, mud, or trees. This part of the human sexuality landscape has been called ecosexuality or sexecology.

These terms were coined by Elizabeth Stephens, a performance artist, activist, and professor, and Annie Sprinkle, a sex-educator and performance artist, and they are fairly new. Ecosexuality often combines art and environmental activism. For some people who practice forms of Earth-based spiritualities, ecosexuality might also include spiritual aspects and practices. Like other areas of sexualities, ecosexuality might be more focused on eroticism or nurturance, or combine both in a range of ways.

(Sexual) roles

The dimensions of eroticism and nurturance also highlight how we might take on different roles to express our sexuality at different times. For example, in some roles we might focus more or less on eroticism or nurturance. A role more focused on nurturance could revolve around wanting to take care of one's partner, for example. This desire might be expressed in a range of ways, which might at times be erotic, such as focusing on their sexual fantasies and wants. The same desire of wanting to take care of one's partner might also be expressed without any eroticism. For example, making a meal or giving a partner a ride might be nurturing—but not erotic—ways of expressing this.

When we engage with others, whether sexually or not, we might take on active or passive roles. We might give or receive, we might make decisions or let other people decide. Sometimes these roles are formalized in practices like kink or BDSM. Kink is an umbrella term used to designate a broad range of sexualities, which include practices that go beyond sexual intercourse. For example, spanking; being aroused by specific body parts, certain fabrics or items of clothing; role-playing; and playing with sensations such as using feathers, or using hot and cold for arousal, could all be described as kinky practices. BDSM is a more specific umbrella term for practices and identities that include bondage and discipline (BD), dominance and submission (DS), and/or sadism and masochism (SM).

Whether or not we engage in kinky and/or BDSM practices, which might include explicitly negotiated roles and power relationships, we all engage in roles when relating to other people. For example, we might be more comfortable with a listener role or a planning role, a decision-making role or a follower role in our relationships.

We often think of some roles as more "extreme" than others. For example, DS (dominant/submissive) roles that are taken on 24/7 in relationships are usually seen as exceptions in dominant cultures. However, other forms of 24/7 relationships, such as marriage, which are also entered by social, cultural, and legal contracts, seem "normal". Similarly, dominant culture seems to have different ways of perceiving topping or bottoming sexually (that is penetrating or being penetrated) very differently if two men are involved compared to a man and a woman. The former might be seen as "unnatural" whereas the latter as "natural". We'll talk much more about these kinds of binaries in the last section of the chapter. First let's consider many different experiences of the landscape of sexuality.

Multiple experiences: A vast landscape of sexualities

- "I like masturbating but I've never felt attracted to another person."
- "I consider myself sapiosexual. What I really find attractive is the way people think."
- "I've been polyamorous for about three decades. There's not a monogamous bone in my body!"
- "I really need to get to know someone before I can even feel any attraction for them. I think of myself as demisexual."
- "There needs to be some sort of power dynamic for me to feel turned on. Without it, nothing happens."
- "I've been married to Jesus for a long time as a lay nun. I find peace and support in prayer."
- "I have romantic feelings for people but I don't have any sexual feelings. My partners and I have a lot of intimacy emotionally and share many values, but we don't have sex."
- "I prefer to date other Black people. There's just too much history with white people and I find trust easier to access when I don't have to worry about racial dynamics as well as sexual ones."
- "I've been a Daddy in kink community for a long time. I love the feeling of taking care of my sub and after-care is really important to me."
- "Swimming is the most sexual activity I can think of. I feel nurtured, held and I love the way water feels on my skin.

It's like water is touching every part of me and I know I am loved."

> *Thought experiment: Where are you in the landscape?*
> *Take a moment to draw the landscape of your sexuality. How do you express your sexuality? Which areas are present in your landscape? How satisfied are you with the ways in which you express your sexuality? Where do you experience eroticism and nurturance, and how? Once you've drawn your landscape, you might want to draw what season it is and what the weather is doing. These represent the influences of cultural, social, physical, religious and/or spiritual norms. How influential are those weather patterns (norms) in your landscape? If you can't draw for any reason, you can do a mindmap, write a description of your sexuality landscape, or simply imagine it.*

1.4 Beyond other sexual binaries

So if we wanted to capture the complexity of our sexuality, we'd have to plot it on multiple dimensions—not just the dimension of the gender/s we're attracted to. We'd also need our locations on those dimensions to be able to move over time for the aspects of our sexuality which are fluid rather than static. Most of us are likely to remain in a pretty similar place on some dimensions, while moving around on others.

Finally, even this multidimensional, shifting model might be limited because dimensions—or spectrums—can easily assume further binaries. For example a spectrum from being attracted to men, to being attracted to women, assumes both that there aren't any further genders we might be attracted to (something we'll explore in the next chapter), and that being more attracted to one gender means being less attracted to the other. The same could be said about a spectrum from submission to dominance:

what about people who are really submissive *and* really dominant? What about people who don't experience either of these things as sexual?

In this last section of the chapter let's take a look at another couple of problematic binaries which underlie a lot of our thinking about sex—normal/abnormal and nature/nurture. Then we'll think about the binaries that distinguish sex from other activities, and whether those are helpful.

The normal/abnormal binary

Perhaps one of the most insidious—and widely accepted—ideas about sex and sexuality is that it's possible—and important—to delineate good, normal, natural sexual identities and practices from those which are bad, abnormal, and unnatural. Some religious leaders, researchers, legislators, medics, and media folks endeavor to do this, drawing the lines between normal and abnormal sex in different ways in different times and places. For example, over our lifetimes "homosexuality" has moved from the "abnormal" to "normal" side of the line, whereas having a high sex drive has perhaps gone in the other direction as it's now often labelled "sex addiction".

Reflection point: Sex lines

Think about all the different forms of sex you're aware of. Which ones are firmly in the "normal" sex category in your wider culture? Which ones are in the "abnormal" one? Are there any you're not sure about? What impact do you think it has on someone if their desires fall into "normal" or "abnormal"?

These lines between normal and abnormal sex tend to be drawn in a couple of different ways, both of which cause many problems.

One way of drawing the line distinguishes "real", "proper", "normal" sex from forms of sex that are seen as somehow inferior. For example, the lists of sexual "disorders" or "dysfunctions" in psychiatric manuals like DSM-5 make it pretty clear that what they mean by "sex" is penis-in-vagina intercourse ending in orgasm. This view filters into sex therapy, self-help, and popular culture meaning that anyone who prefers other kinds of sex—all or some of the time—can easily feel inferior.

Ironically this is actually likely to lead to *more* sexual problems, and even non-consensual sex, happening, as people try to conform to the "right" kind of sex and the "right" amount of sex in their relationships, rather than tuning into what they actually enjoy. It's hard to be present to the experience you're having if you feel like you have to have an orgasm in order to be having "normal sex". It's difficult to enjoy oral sex or mutual masturbation if you've been taught that it's only "foreplay" and not "the real thing". And why is solo sex generally seen as somehow lesser—or more suspicious—than sex with other people when it can be one of the greatest pleasures many people enjoy?

The other way the line between normal and abnormal sex is drawn separates "proper" sex from sex which is seen as risky or dangerous. For example, sex advice books often save "spicy" or "kinky" sex for the final chapter, and stick a load of health warnings around it as if being tied up or spanking somebody is inherently more likely to lead to harm than penis-in-vagina sex. Again psychiatric manuals have whole lists of "paraphilias", many of which are things that it's perfectly possible to enjoy consensually like dressing up, or taking dominant or submissive roles during sex.

These lines lead to a lot of guilt and shame around sex, especially given that kinky fantasies are hugely common—just look at the popularity of *Fifty Shades of Grey*. Again this can mean that many people are never sexually fulfilled because they can't bring themselves to admit to their desires. Or it can mean that people *do* try to bring kink into their sex life, but in ways that aren't as safe or consensual as they should be because they're too embarrassed to communicate openly about it.

Gayle Rubin is an author we both admire who has written extensively on the problem with the normal/abnormal binary. She suggests that we could judge the quality of sex more by how consensual it is and/or how pleasurable or fulfilling it is for the people involved. This quote from Rubin is a good one to return to you if you find yourself judging the sex that you—or another person—enjoys:

> Most people find it difficult to grasp that whatever they like to do sexually will be thoroughly repulsive to someone else, and that whatever repels them sexually will be the most treasured delight of someone, somewhere... Most people mistake their sexual preferences for a universal system that will or should work for everyone.[5]

The nature/nurture binary
As Rubin points out, the types of sex and sexuality which are commonly assumed to be more normal are also often assumed to be the *good* kinds of sex, and the kinds of sex that are *natural*. By "natural" we might think of biological urges that we can't help, or the type of sex we would find among non-human animals, for example.

There are many things to question in this conflation of binaries: good/bad, with normal/abnormal, and natural/unnatural. First off, can we really say that "normal" and "natural" things are somehow morally better than those that are "abnormal" or "unnatural"?

---

5   Rubin, G. (1984) "Thinking Sex: Notes for a Radical Theory of the Politics of Sexuality." In C.S. Vance (ed.) *Pleasure and Danger: Exploring Female Sexuality.* London: Pandora, p.283.

It's not normal to be a genius, a musical prodigy, or a great altruist, but we generally don't shun those people! And it's pretty unnatural to use smartphones and to fly around the world, yet people welcome the ability to do those things.

Often when normal and natural arguments are made around sex and sexuality they are just wrong. For example, people argue that penis-in-vagina sex is more natural because it's what animals do, ignoring all the huge amount of "same sex" sex, mutual masturbation, oral sex, and so on that happen in the animal world. People argue that monogamy is the normal way to do relationships, despite the larger number of cultures—and people—globally who practice some form of non-monogamy.

But when we point out these errors we're at risk of slipping right back into the same assumption: that something being common, normal, or natural is somehow better. Should somebody whose erotic desires are very rare really be judged compared to somebody whose desires are run-of-the-mill? Why should it matter? Similarly, why do we care whether somebody's sexuality is "caused" by some biological variation, or by their life experiences, by the culture around them, or by choices they have made? Again, if they're acting consensually, and finding pleasure or fulfillment, why should we care?

But we do seem to care a lot. A huge amount of time, energy, and resources are put into scientific research to determine whether various aspects of sexuality are down to "nature" or "nurture": the search for the gay gene, for example, or attempts to find "natural" differences between what men and women are into sexually by wiring them up to probes and showing them various kinds of pornography.

Again the binary here is a big problem. We know that even pretty simple human activities can't be simply divided into "nature" or "nurture". They're generally a complex combination of the way our bodies and brains work (biological), our experiences and the choices we make in life (psychological), and the messages we receive from the world around us, and the possibilities wider culture opens up or closes down for us (social). For example, these possibilities around sex and sexuality often differ according to how we—and others—see our gender, race, class, age, or disability, something we'll discuss further in Chapter 4. Different people are seen as more or less sexual, and more or less sexually attractive, in wider culture due to these—and other—intersecting identities and experiences.

The word "biopsychosocial" captures this multiplicity and the way in which all of these aspects impact each other in hugely complex feedback loops. If something as straightforward as riding a bike works in this way, then surely it must be true of something as complex as our sexualities.

Binaries between sex and other activities

A final set of sex binaries that are useful to look at are those we draw—or don't draw—between sex and other things. For example, asexual and aromantic people have helpfully highlighted the way that people often assume that sexual attraction and romantic attraction go together. Actually for some people these things mesh (they're attracted to the same people sexually and romantically) and for some they don't. Some people experience both sexual attraction and romantic attraction, some neither, and some experience one without the other. Any of these combinations is just fine.

Kinksters have helpfully challenged the lines we draw between sex and other practices, for example leisure, play, spirituality, and healing. Many kinky activities don't require any of the things that we commonly associate with sex in order to be enjoyable. There may be a climax of sensation or experience that isn't an orgasm, or no climax at all. There may be no genital contact, or even no physical contact. We can ask ourselves whether an adult role-playing being a baby or a puppy falls under our definition of sex, or is something more like play. There is a lot of similarity between some kink practices like piercing or flagellation and aesthetic or religious rituals.

You could say that the sex/not-sex line is an important one because it's necessary to delineate appropriate from inappropriate behavior—in a workplace environment for example. But again we would argue that consent is the more useful concept to consider here. Is everybody fully informed about what's going on? Is everyone involved able to provide consent and legally of an age at which they can do so? Is it clear enough that they can choose to participate or not, or ask for more information? What are the power dynamics in play, and how possible is it for consent to happen given these dynamics?

> ### Thought experiment: Expanding your erotic imagination
> *Alone, or with friends, try noting down every sexual, sensual, or erotic activity you can think of that might be the most "treasured delight of someone, somewhere", as Gayle Rubin put it. Writing them all on post-it notes is a great way to do it because then you can move them around. When you've come up with everything you can, think about which ones your wider culture tends to "count" as sex, and which it doesn't; which are seen as normal or abnormal.*
>
> *For yourself you can organize these activities into piles of "yes", "no", or "maybe" to get more of a sense of what you might like to try. Feel into what it's like to imagine engaging in each one. Of course we can't step outside of culture, so it's useful to consider how much your responses are about what you find exciting—or not—and how much they're about what others might think, how these things are viewed in wider culture, or what is regarded as possible for someone of your intersecting gender, class, race, age, body, and so on to engage in (see Chapter 4). Remember biopsychosocial—it's probably a complex combination of all these things.*

Audre Lorde's brilliant essay "Uses of the Erotic"[6] is useful to expand out what we think of as erotic way beyond what's sexual. She says that the erotic is a vital source of power and information in our lives, but that it gets warped by the way our culture views sex. When we're taught so much to fear straying into "abnormal" sex, and to make ourselves have sex that we don't really want in order to prove that we're "normal", we teach ourselves to fear our erotic desires and urges, both in relation to sex and more widely than this.

Lorde argues that this gets in the way of us being able to tune into how we're feeling across many aspects of our lives, so we find it hard to allow ourselves—for example—to pursue other kinds of relationships that might be nourishing for us, or the kinds of work and play that we'd really find fulfilling and stimulating. She says that the erotic is seen as dangerous in our society because it would mean that we "demand from ourselves and from our life-pursuits that they feel in accordance with that joy which we know ourselves to be capable of".[7] This means not settling "for the convenient, the shoddy, the conventionally expected, nor the merely safe".[8] Perhaps that is why the erotic tends to be limited to sex, and then policed in all the ways we've discussed in this chapter.

Further Resources

You can read more about bisexuality, pansexuality, queer sexualities, and beyond in the following books:

- Amherst, M. (2018) *Go the Way Your Blood Beats*. London: Repeater Books.

---

6   Lorde, A. (1984/2012) "Uses of the Erotic: The Erotic as Power." In A. Lorde (ed.) *Sister Outsider: Essays and Speeches.* New York: Crossing Press.

7   Lorde (1984/2012), p.90.

8   Lorde, p.90.

- Anderlini-D'Onofrio, S. and Hagamen, L. (2015) *Eco-sexuality: When Nature Inspires the Arts of Love*. CreateSpace Independent Publishing Platform.
- Barker, M-J. (2018) *The Psychology of Sex*. London: Routledge and Psychology Press.
- Barker, M-J. and Scheele, J. (2016) *Queer: A Graphic History*. London: Icon Books.
- Eisner, S. (2013) *Bi: Notes for a Bisexual Revolution*. Berkeley, CA: Seal Press.
- Harrad, K. (ed.) (2016) *Purple Prose: Bisexuality in Britain*. Portland, OR: Thorntree Press LLC.
- Roche, J. (2018) *Queer Sex*. London: Jessica Kingsley Publishers.
- Taormino, T. (ed.) (2012) *The Ultimate Guide to Kink: BDSM, Role Play and the Erotic Edge*. Jersey City, NJ: Cleis Press.

These are the other books we mentioned in the chapter:

- Diamond, L.M. (2008) *Sexual Fluidity*. Cambridge, MA: Harvard University Press.
- Sedgwick, E.K. (1990) *Epistemology of the Closet*. Oakland, CA: University of California Press.
- Ward, J. (2015) *Not Gay: Sex between Straight White Men*. New York: NYU Press.

These two essays mentioned in the chapter are also brilliant:

- Rubin, G. (1984) 'Thinking Sex: Notes for a Radical Theory of the Politics of Sexuality.' In C.S. Vance (ed.) *Pleasure and Danger: Exploring Female Sexuality*. London: Pandora.
- Lorde, A. (1984/2012) 'Uses of the Erotic: The Erotic as Power.' In A. Lorde (ed.) *Sister Outsider: Essays and Speeches*. New York: Crossing Press.

To apply these ideas more to your own sexuality and sex life, check these out:

- Barker, M-J. and Hancock, J. (2017) *Enjoy Sex (How, When and If You Want To): A Practical and Inclusive Guide.* London: Icon Books.
- Barker, M-J. and Hancock, J. (2017) *Understanding ourselves through erotic fantasies.* Available from: megjohnandjustin. com/publications
- Iantaffi, A., Barker, M-J., van Anders, S. and Scheele, J. (2018) *Mapping your sexuality: From sexual orientation to sexual configurations theory.* Available at www.rewriting-the-rules. com/wp-content/uploads/2018/08/MappingYourSexuality. pdf, accessed on 21 November 2018.

If you want to know more about bi and queer matters, these website are great:

- The Bisexual Index: bisexualindex.org.uk
- The Bisexual Resource Center: biresource.org
- Bi Community News: bicommunitynews.co.uk
- Bis of color: bisofcolour.tumblr.com
- Biscuit Magazine: thisisbiscuit.co.uk
- The Queerness: thequeerness.com
- AVEN: asexuality.org

If you're interested in ecosexuality, this sexually explicit video, "Holy Mother I'd Like to Fuck", by Pavini Moray is a celebration of it: vimeo.com/ondemand/holymilf

CHAPTER 2

Genders

In the last chapter we touched on the point that one major problem with binary models of sexual "orientation"—where you're oriented towards men or towards women—is that gender itself isn't binary in this way. Even Kinsey and Klein-type scales which measure sexuality on a spectrum from "same-gender" to "opposite-gender" attraction are problematic because they assume two—and only two—genders.

The non-binary nature of gender is even less publicly accepted than the non-binary nature of sexuality. Indeed many authors who write about bisexuality or queer still refer to bi or queer "men and women" only. The gender binary is—if anything—even more deeply rooted in white western dominant culture than the sexuality binary, although they are intrinsically linked. Being seen as a "real" man or women is often significantly defined by attraction and desirability to the "opposite" gender. And men and women who are attracted to the same gender are often stereotyped as being feminine men or masculine women.

We can see that gender is not inevitably binary when we look back through time and around the world today. When we do, we see many other ways of understanding gender, some of which are based on the idea of a singular gender, some on many genders, and some on the idea that gender simply isn't that significant. The gender binary is culturally specific and—like the sexuality binary—related to the settler-colonial, imperialist project of categorizing different groups of people and bodies as superior or inferior to each other. It's also rooted in a capitalist system which required femininity to be "opposite" to masculinity in various ways in order to justify women's unpaid labour within the home: caring for the current workforce and raising the next one, or—particularly in the case of women of color—serving other people's families in these ways.

In this chapter we'll look in more depth at the binary sex/gender system and why it is so questionable, also touching on the reasons why regarding sex—but not gender—as binary isn't the answer. We'll then say more about people who experience—and identify—their gender as non-binary and how this might be useful for all of us in understanding our genders. After that we'll consider two other binaries which are increasingly used to make sense of gender, but which should be scrutinized just as critically as we scrutinize the man/woman binary. Those are the binary between trans and cisgender people, and the binary/non-binary binary! Don't worry if that last binary makes your brain hurt, we'll take it gently.

2.1 The sex/gender binary

When Alex used to be pregnant, one of the most frequent questions they were asked—besides if it was okay for complete strangers to touch their belly—was whether they were expecting a "boy or a girl". People seemed confused when they happily declared that they were hoping for a baby hippo, but that it was probably a tiny human they were growing. This is not an unusual scenario as this question is often asked of pregnant people.

If we gently pointed out that people are asking to know what the genitals of an unborn baby are so that they can non-consensually classify them according to an arbitrary and scientifically incorrect system of sex and gender, they would probably be confused, or even angry. Sex and gender can indeed be confusing terms, with a range of meanings. For many people sex/gender is also its own binary.

Many think of sex as pertaining to biological characteristics, such as genitals and secondary sex characteristics, and of gender as being a purely historical, cultural, and social construct. We—the authors—believe this is a false binary and that sex and gender are related, yet distinct, and not a binary in their own right. We unpack this briefly in this section. However, there's much more to discuss here than space in this chapter allows. Fortunately we've already written a whole book about it: *How to Understand Your Gender: A Practical Guide for Exploring Who You Are.* That book is meant for people of all genders and, if you're interested, we invite you to check it out as we go into much more depth into the topic there than we can here!

Defining sex

Sex, as we said, can be a confusing word. It can mean an act we do by ourselves or with other people, if we mean having sex. However it can also refer to the binary male/female for humans, non-human animals, and plants. In this section, we stay focused on human animals. However, the plant and animal worlds also have many ways to reproduce that have nothing to do with sexual dimorphism—that is having two sexes: male/female of the same species, with distinct characteristics.

In dominant culture, we usually think of sex as binary and being associated with genitals. This idea is called gender essentialism and it goes back to some Greek ideas expressed by Plato and then picked up by Christianity. Basically sex is seen as male/female, and it is assigned on the basis of which genitals we were born with. If we're born with a vagina then we're assigned female, and if we're born with a penis then we're assigned male. This is viewed by some as an unalienable fact.

However, the reality is that our sex is not just determined by our genitals and the secondary sex characteristics that develop in puberty. Our chromosomes also determine what our sex is. Given that very few people will have their chromosomal makeup analyzed, it seems fair to say that the sex we're assigned at birth is an approximation based on visible characteristics, rather than an objective account of our biology.

The existence of intersex people seems to challenge the male/female binary for sex. Please note that we're still talking about sex as a biological dimension here and not gender. We know that this can be confusing because these terms are so often used interchangeably in dominant culture.

Intersex is an umbrella category for people born with sexual and/or reproductive anatomy that doesn't fit with the sexual dimorphism of male/female. For some people, their intersex status is visible from birth, and for others it's not. Some intersex people might even never find out that they're intersex. Intersex people are not trans people, even though some intersex people might also identify as trans.

This distinction is important because people sometimes get confused, and might even "use" intersex people as "evidence" that gender is not binary, and to support the existence of trans people. We would say that the existence of trans people is evidence of their existence (yes, that is a tautology and we unpack it in a moment), and that the existence of intersex people troubles the idea of sex, not gender, as a purely binary system of male/female.

Many intersex activists have also been clear on how they're impacted differently by the male/female sex binary, compared to trans people. For example, many intersex babies have historically received unnecessary surgeries, so that they could grow up not knowing their intersex status and "fitting in" with cultural and societal expectations. It has taken extensive and global activism by intersex people and some of their families to begin to change these oppressive and harmful medical practices. These practices are also rooted in binary ideas of gender, to which we now turn.

Defining gender

Gender can be defined as a complex biopsychosocial construct. What this means is that there are biological, psychological, and social components of gender, which are in relationship and which interact with one another in complex ways. Let's unpack that a little.

Biological aspects of gender might refer to how our brain works, what hormones are being produced by our body, and how the two interact. Of course this is a little tricky as we know that the brain and hormones are responsive to both environment and activities. Feminist scientists, like Sari van Anders and Cordelia Fine, have, for example, shown how our hormonal levels and neural pathways might change depending on which activities we take part in, as well as the environment around us.

Psychological aspects refer to how we might experience our gender, that is our felt sense of gender: the way we identify our gender, how it feels when we put certain clothes on, which mannerisms feel most comfortable, and how we think about our own gender. Of course all of these are connected to both biological aspects as well as social ones.

Social aspects of gender focus on how gender is played out in a specific historical, geographical, and cultural moment. What expectations do people around us have of specific genders? What are the gendered norms around clothing, activities, mannerisms, social roles, and so on? Once again, and by this point unsurprisingly, these too are related to biological and psychological components.

When we say that gender is biopsychosocial, what we mean to indicate is the complex web of relationships and interactions that occur within and between these domains. We cannot consider each one of them separately because they all influence each other in various ways.

Furthermore, sex and gender also interface. For example, if people are assigned a certain sex at birth and identify with a gender that is considered congruent with that sex assigned at birth culturally, they are cisgender—that is their sex assigned at birth and gender identity are on the same side (from the Latin prefix "cis"). If someone identifies as a gender that is not congruent with the sex they were assigned at birth, they are transgender—that is their sex assigned at birth and gender identity are not on the same side, they are across (from the Latin "trans"). More about the cis/trans binary in section 2.3 of this chapter.

Gender has its own man/woman binary, to which we return later. In dominant culture, in fact, as well as assuming that sex is a binary, and using sex and gender interchangeably, we also often assume that gender is binary. The existence of trans and/or non-binary people troubles this binary. However, the man/woman binary does not work for anyone, including cisgender people.

For example, what do we mean exactly when we say someone is a man or a woman? We'd say that we're referring to norms that are historically, geographically, culturally, and socially determined. We might also be referring to biological markers, but those are always being read through cultural and social lenses. This is complicated for at least two reasons. First of all, when we talk about gender—this large biopsychosocial construct—what are we referring to when applying it to the individual?

Are we talking about someone's:

- gender identity, that is the sense of who they are
- gender role, that is how they interact with the world around them according to gender norms
- gender expression, that is how they're manifesting their gender through clothes, mannerisms, hairstyle, and so on
- gender experience, that is how they're navigating the world because of their gender?

The other reason why this is complicated is that gender cannot be defined as being outside of—and separate from—other identity categories and experiences, such as Indigeneity, race, ethnicity, disability, sexuality, class, age, citizenship, religion, or spirituality (see Chapter 4). Our gender interacts with all these other aspects of ourselves, both on individual and collective levels.

Our bodies are not just gendered by others but also racialized in specific ways. The experiences of white women are very different than the experiences of Asian women, for example. The latter are often seen as submissive, and both innocent and hypersexual at the same time in Western dominant culture, and represented as such in movies, TV, and books, because of *both* their gender and race, at the same time.

The simple binary man/woman is therefore inadequate to identify the multitudes of identities, roles, expressions, and experiences that people inhabit as we'll see shortly. Before we move on though, let's take a moment to think about gender a little bit more.

Thought experiment: The many aspects of gender
Over the next few days observe how gender is everywhere. You can
consider books, songs, TV and movie characters, adverts, magazines,
and social media, for example. You may want to take some notes as
your observations unfold. Take time to notice gendered interactions,
or when gender language is used. For example, if someone addresses
someone else as madam or sir, or daughter, or boyfriend. If somebody
holds a door open for another person, or who a server gives the bill
to at a restaurant when there is more than one adult at the table.
Notice if things in shops and ads are categorized and/or marketed
according to gender.

Once you've made a few observations, take time to think whether
your observations are about gender in terms of someone's identity,
expression, role or experiences, or whether they're about social and
cultural expectations, or a mixture of several aspects. Take time to
reflect on whether there are other factors at play in the interactions
as well, such as age, class, disability, race, ethnicity, sexuality, and so
on. We invite you to undertake this exercise from a place of curiosity,
non-judgment of yourself and others, and kindness. Once you're done,
you may want to reflect on what difference what you've learned
might make in your life moving forward.

2.2 Non-binary genders

We—your authors—are both non-binary. What does that mean?
Non-binary is an umbrella term for all the gender expressions,
identities, and experiences that fall outside of the binary gender
system that we described in the previous section. Some people
prefer the umbrella terms NB, enby, or genderqueer because they'd
rather not be defined by what they are not. Others prefer more
specific terms, or not to use a label at all.

We'll use the term non-binary here as it seems to be the most widely used one at the moment, but we'll also be mindful of some of the limitations with it, just as we were with bisexuality in the previous chapter. A good way of moving away from binary thinking is to ask *both* what terms like these open up *and* what they close down, rather than uncritically accepting or rejecting them in their entirety. We'll come back to non-binary thinking many times during the rest of this book.

As we've already seen, in Western cultures people tend to be assigned male or female from before birth—when the doctor announces "it's a girl" or "it's a boy". This means that non-binary folks are also trans: they haven't remained in the sex/gender they were assigned at birth. However, not all non-binary people identify as trans. Some associate being trans with medical interventions—some or all of which they might not want to engage in (just as some trans women and men do and do not). Some don't identify as trans because they also question the cis/trans binary which we'll come on to shortly, or because it would be too unsafe for them to be out as trans, or for other reasons.

Reflection point: Non-binaryness

Where are you at in relation to non-binary gender? Are there any aspects of your gender identity, expression, or experience which seem to be closer to a gender other than the one people tend to see you as? If so, what words would you use to describe this? How do you feel about it?

The non-binary umbrella

Like the categories of "man" or "woman", "non-binary" encompasses a vast range of different ways of identifying, expressing, and experiencing gender. Here's what it means for us, your authors.

Alex writes…

My sense of gender has definitely changed over time. At one point, I did identify as genderqueer, but when the term non-binary started to become more visible, it just made so much more sense to me. I feel that my gender and sexuality are closely intertwined. I'm a femme trans masculine queer person and I use both he and they pronouns. I know that this can sound complicated but, basically, I imagine that if I had been born a cis boy, I would have presented as a femme kind of man, and I would have been mostly gay (but probably still attracted to masculine people of all genders). Some of my gender expressions and many of my mannerisms are definitely more feminine than masculine, but I also like to present as masculine in my day-to-day life, as that feels more like me. When I used to identify and present as "girl" and later "woman", it never felt like me. Non-binary makes sense because there are all these sides of me that just don't fit into a neat binary box.

MJ writes…

For me being non-binary is about embracing multiple sides of myself which are differently gendered. I like my non-binary pronoun "they" not just because it is gender neutral, but also because it can be used in both the singular and the plural sense. I experience myself as pretty plural. Being non-binary enables me to embrace the more masculine sides of myself which I was discouraged from expressing as I was growing up. My gender is definitely a work in progress. As I learn to understand and embody these different sides of myself the overall "me" gradually shifts and changes in exciting—and sometimes challenging—ways.

And of course, other people's non-binary experience is completely different from ours. Let's hear from a few of them:

Multiple experiences: Non-binary genders

- "My gender feels somewhere at the midpoint on a spectrum between masculine and feminine. I guess you could say androgynous, but people generally associate that with skinny white people and I'm a proud, fat black person so it's not a great fit. I'm me-gender."

- "I'd say I was a demiboy. I feel like I am masculine of centre but gender isn't a strong thing for me, more muted."

- "I use the word bigender. That means that sometimes I feel male and sometimes I feel female. I wear different clothes and things depending on how I feel on that particular day. Some of my friends know to use different names for me too which really helps. Genderfluid is another word that's a good fit for me."

- "As a two spirit person my gender is distinct from womanhood or manhood and I can trace it back through the generations in my Native community. It's not just about gender though. Two spirit captures a combination of what you might call gender, sexuality, and spirituality."

- "I'm agender which means I don't have a gender. I hate it when people say 'oh everyone has a gender'. I really don't experience myself as gendered in any way."

- "I'm femme. People often struggle to see that as a non-binary gender, particularly because I was assigned female at birth, but for me it's about pointing out how all gender is something we perform. I also like the word genderqueer because it gets at how gender is political as well as personal for me."

So being under the non-binary umbrella means that you're likely to share some things with other non-binary people, as well as having many differences from them. Again this is a *both/and* thing rather than it being that non-binary people are *either* all the same, *or* completely different to each other. This understanding is important because hopefully it prevents us from trying to distinguish the "real", "proper" non-binary people from those who aren't. We'll touch on these kinds of hierarchies of transness or queerness in the next section.

When we talk with other non-binary people, we're often struck that most of us share experiences like:

- everyday misgendering (being read as a gender which doesn't fit with our sense of ourselves)
- moments of gender dysphoria and/or euphoria (when we feel a negative sense of our bodies and experiences not fitting our sense of ourselves, or a positive sense of them fitting well)
- the hugely positive impact when we are actually *seen* by others in the way we see ourselves, or the world is arranged in ways that allow for our gender (like gender neutral toilets, or non-gendered announcements on the train).

But we're equally struck by the massive diversity in how we experience, identify, and express our genders, for example:

- For some of us it's vital to make bodily changes to bring our outer appearance in line with our inner experience; for others it isn't important, or we actively wouldn't want to make such changes.
- Some of us want to be read in specific ways by others; others want people to struggle to read us in gendered ways at all.
- We've all come from different places genderwise and are heading in different directions, which give us very

different relationships with femininity, masculinity, and our
non-binary-ness.

These differences make it clear how other identities and aspects
of our lives can be as important as—or more important than—
gender, and how they intersect with gender in such complex ways
that it would be impossible to disentangle them. For example,
our race, ethnicity, class, culture, and faith background, and the
geographical location we grew up in, all open up and close down
different gender possibilities, which can impact how we experience
our genders through our lives (see Chapter 4).

The non-binary movement

The non-binary movement—or community—is relatively recent in
comparison with many sexuality and gender movements. But now
it's here, it's moving very fast. It may well have moved on between
the time that we write this and the time that you read it. And of
course it's also plural rather than singular because in reality there
are many different non-binary online groups, activist collectives,
community settings, and so on, all of which may feed into each
other and overlap, or be relatively separate.

In places like the UK and US it's a pretty new thing to be
able to identify yourself as non-binary, and it's still not possible
on many documents and in many public spaces. Non-binary
activist Nat Titman studied all the UK surveys where people
could identify as something other than just "male" or "female" and
found 1 in 250 people identified in that way when they were given
the chance.[1] But Daphna Joel and colleagues found that over a

---

1   https://practicalandrogyny.com/2014/12/16/how-many-people-in-the-uk-
    are-nonbinary/

third of people actually experience themselves as being—to some extent—"the other gender", "both genders", or "neither gender".[2] So the proportion of non-binary people is somewhere between 0.4 percent and 35 percent! This is pretty similar to the differences we saw between people *identifying* as bisexual, and *experiencing* attraction to more than one gender in the previous chapter.

Currently being non-binary in Western countries is also not a binary good *or* bad experience. There are moves to recognize genders beyond the binary and to give non-binary people rights and protections under the law, at the same time as there's at least equally as strong a move to hold onto the binary gender system very tightly. On the positive side, for example, Facebook now offers over 50 gender terms and non-binary they pronouns. In 2016 the *National Geographic* brought out an issue on the "gender revolution", which covered non-binary gender very seriously. There is a non-binary character on the mainstream TV show *Billions* played by a non-binary actor. Also several stores have stopped gendering the toys or clothes that they sell.

On the other hand, we are subject to endless media "debates" about whether non-binary gender even exists. There are frequent attacks on charities which support trans and non-binary people, as well as battles over providing gender neutral toilets. Also "gender reveal" parties and videos are becoming increasingly common, despite seemingly locking kids into the binary gender from an early age. Parents who do not gender their children from the start tend to be attacked and accused of abuse. There is no legal recognition of non-binary genders in most places.

---

2   Joel, D., Tarrasch, R., Berman, Z., Mukamel, M. and Ziv, E. (2014) "Queering gender: studying gender identity in 'normative' individuals." *Psychology & Sexuality* 5, 4, 291–321.

LIFE ISN'T BINARY

Slow down!

Phew, that was a lot! Let's take a breather, shall we?

In fact, let's use our breath to make a sound. We'd like to invite you to "voo".

Take a moment to get comfortable, either in your seat, or standing, with your knees soft and not locked in place. The idea is to breathe in deeply, as if you're breathing up from the earth, then, as you breathe out, make the sound VOO for as long as your breath allows.

If you run out of voice before you run out of breath, keep breathing out, until it's time to breathe in again. Do this three to four times.

We're going for a foghorn type of sound, so that there is some vibration in your body.It doesn't need to be pretty!

Once you're done vooing, notice how you feel.

Do you feel the same or different? Was this experience pleasant, unpleasant, or neutral? Then, when you're ready, the book awaits.

68

2.3 Beyond the cis/trans binary

Non-binary genders seem to be troubling to both some trans and cis people. In many ways, non-binary genders do, in fact, trouble the cis/trans binary. If, as we explore in the next section, lines cannot be easily drawn, what even happens to the cis/trans binary? This is what we address in this section.

In some ways, the cis/trans binary seems straightforward: at one pole are the people whose sex assigned at birth aligns with their gender identity, that is cis people; at the other are the people whose sex assigned at birth does not align with their gender identity, that is trans people. Both categories include several gender expressions, roles, and experiences, but the two main umbrellas seem pretty clear, right? At this point you might have noticed that for us none of this is so simple or so binary! Let's take a closer look.

The "true transsexual" dominant narrative

Historically the cis/trans binary seems to be partially born out of how the medical system would deal with trans people. Given that, within Western dominant discourse, being trans has not always been seen as just part of the range of gender identities in humans, several researchers and medical practitioners set out to ensure that trans people who could not be "trained out" of their trans identities, could at least become as close to cis people as possible.

Changing a trans person's body, name, appearance, and legal status seemed to be the only "logical" solution to medical professionals, and to many trans people too. There just did not seem to be any other plausible alternatives if trans people were to live somewhat comfortably in dominant culture. However, how were the medical professionals to separate the "true transsexual"—who was willing to even risk their lives for procedures that, now routine, were unknown and potentially lethal at the time—from people who were merely "playing" with their gender, maybe because of their sexuality?

This is one of the ways in which the "true transsexual" narrative emerges. Now, let's be clear, we're not saying that body modification is not necessary. It is vital for many of us. Trans people have every right to have access to legal, medical, and social transition processes. However, for several decades, all trans people were required to "prove" that they were "true transsexuals", if they wanted access to any of these processes.

Even though this is no longer the case, and trans and/or non-binary people can access services with a little more ease some of the time, the "true transsexual" narrative persists within trans communities and medical communities and in dominant culture. For example, it underlies the fear that some professionals and members of the public alike seem to harbor around trans adolescents accessing medical services, or younger children accessing social transition processes or, at an appropriate stage of development, puberty blockers.

The "true transsexual" narrative means that often trans people may doubt themselves. Are they really trans if they do not experience dysphoria all the time? Are they really "trans enough" if they don't want to change their name, or maybe even their appearance? The "true transsexual" narrative draws a clear line in the sand not only between trans and cis people, with a firm binary understanding of who belongs where, but also between trans people—separating "true transsexuals" from "transgender" people. This, of course, creates another binary transsexual/transgender, which, as far as we understand, has only ever served the maintenance of the same cisgenderist system under which we all suffer, regardless of gender identity.

Who is trans enough?

As stated, many trans people end up feeling as if they might not be "trans enough" to ask people to use other pronouns, or a different name, or to access life-saving services. Alex, for example, used to work at a gender identity clinic in the US. It was common for them to come across well-rehearsed stories, especially by young people, who felt they had to tell the dominant narrative of "having always known" that they "were born in the wrong body", in order to access desperately needed services. Because of their own trans and non-binary status, Alex was usually able to reassure clients that it was okay to tell their lived experience, and that they would not be "punished" by being denied services for being authentic.

We know now that there are as many different ways of being trans as there are of being cis, because we have listened to so many people share their pain around gender, no matter what their identity. However, if wider culture maintains the trans/cis binary, it can also maintain cisgenderism—that is the ideology that places being cis as more "natural and normal" than being trans. Maintaining cisgenderism as a dominant ideology also supports dominant understandings of sexuality as binary, as discussed in Chapter 1: that is gay/straight. In fact this ideology was so strong that in some countries trans people were, and sometimes still are, required to divorce their spouse of the opposite gender and undergo sterilization before they were allowed access to transition services.

If the cis/trans binary holds then other binaries such as straight/gay, man/woman can also remain undisturbed in dominant culture. These binaries then uphold a hierarchy where cis (white) straight men can be at the top, followed by cis (white) straight women, then maybe cis (white) gay men and so on. The status quo can continue without too much upheaval. Therefore, maintaining a narrative, within trans communities, that there's a right way to be trans otherwise you're cis, serves the same cis, settler-colonial, racist, patriarchal, heteronormative, ableist system that keeps us all oppressed, as we discuss further in Chapter 4 when we take a closer look at binaries around bodies.

Reflection point: Who decides who is trans?

What would you say defines a person as cis or trans? Where is the line that should not be crossed? For example, if someone likes to crossdress for parties and sexual play, can they identify as trans? If not, why not? Who decides who is trans and who is not? Is it cis people or trans people? If it is trans people, are there some trans people who have "more rights" than others to determine who is "trans enough"? If so, what are the characteristics of the trans people who can determine who can identify as trans? If the same person who enjoys crossdressing wants to identify as cis, can they do so? Who decides whether it's okay or not?

The cis dominant narrative

We've started addressing the "true transsexual" and "trans enough" narratives. However, there's another cis dominant narrative that contributes to maintaining the trans/cis binary in dominant culture. This narrative holds that cis people have always known their gender identity and have never questioned it. Cis men, for example, generally do not crossdress unless it is for "fun", and as a way of denigrating trans women by implying they're "men in dresses" and, as such, unattractive. Similarly, cis women who crossdress as masculine are considered unattractive within dominant culture and are usually read as lesbians.

A cis dominant narrative also maintains the idea that cis genders are static and fixed, and that there are no changes or transitions over time, be they legal, medical, or social. TV documentaries and other media tend to sensationalize trans bodies and lives by framing our stories in a "freak of the week" format, which acts like we're totally weird for making social and physical changes. In contrast, cis people make social and physical changes to their genders all the time without much fanfare.

For example, many cis people legally change their names when they get married, or use nicknames, which may or may not be related to their given names. Many cis people have medical interventions to better conform to historical, cultural, and social gendered beauty standards, such as rhinoplasties or chest reconstruction surgeries. Cis men might want to reduce breast tissue if they have gynecomastia or pseudogynecomastia, whereas cis women might want to reduce or increase the size of their breasts. Cis women might also undergo vaginal rejuvenation procedures, as well as a broad range of procedures to conform to body ideals.

Cis people might also take hormones for a variety of reasons. They may change their appearance, grow or cut their hair, start wearing completely different styles of clothes, and change their gender roles over time. For example, someone might go from being a stay-at-home parent to running their own business and taking on the role of main breadwinner. Cis people's genders might also be perceived differently as they age. Many cis women have written and spoken about the loss of erotic capital—that is the social value that is linked to being considered sexually attractive—as they get older and how that impacts them both in their personal and professional lives.

Despite the fact that both cis and trans people might share gendered experiences and transitions, the cis/trans binary ensures that they're kept divided and that trans narratives are seen as "sensational" and "exceptional", whereas cis narratives appear to be "normal" and "common". What would happen if we could get away—or at least challenge—the cis/trans binary? What becomes possible when we look at our relationship with gender as being potentially more fluid than we thought and capable of changing over time?

What would happen if it were not a big deal to discover that someone is trans, or if we just stopped assuming that we can actually identify who is trans or cis without asking them? What would happen if we could all recognize the many ways in which people can relate to their genders? In the next section we explore the binary/non-binary binary and continue to unravel the ways in which binaries want to cut us up in gendered groups. Before we move on though, here are some brief stories of people who didn't feel cis or trans enough.

Multiple experiences: Not...enough.

- "I've never liked the way people looked at me because of my chest. I hated having large breasts, just hated it. When I had a breast reduction, it was as if a weight had been lifted off me. I could go around without getting stared at, or worse grabbed. I could also wear more fitted clothes, which I prefer, more easily. I felt like I could finally see me, the way I wanted to be in my head."

- "When I was diagnosed with prostate cancer, one of my worst fears was losing my ability to have erections. I started asking myself whether I could even be a man. Now, it feels silly. I'm just glad I'm alive. I love my life with my wife, and my children. I can't believe how much power I gave to this part of me before. I have discovered that being a man is so much more than being able to have erections without any support."

- "I love being penetrated. I never wanted bottom surgery. I'm a gay trans man and I love my bonus hole. My therapist didn't believe I was trans for a long time. Even I started questioning it. After all, if I didn't want a penis and I was happy having sex with men, why did I want to transition? But I knew that I just didn't want to have sex with men. I wanted to have sex with men as a man. Just because I don't have genital dysphoria, it doesn't mean I'm not trans".

- "I never had a period and I couldn't have children. For a long time I felt that I couldn't be a 'real woman' without these experiences. Now I've made my peace. But it still hurts when people make grand statements about 'all women bleed' or equate womanhood with motherhood. My womanhood has never been about my reproduction because that never worked."

- "I have a condition that makes it impossible for me to take hormones or have bottom surgery. For some time I felt I could not live in the world as a trans woman without these things. However, as I met other trans women who did not take hormones or had no surgical intervention, I became bolder. I couldn't bear the thought of living as a man just because my health was compromised. I am a trans woman, no matter what anyone else says."

2.4 Beyond the binary/non-binary binary

So now we get to the complicated part. If we're going to question the gay/straight binary, and the man/woman binary, and the trans/cis binary—and we *should*—then surely we can't, in good conscience, hold tight to a new binary between non-binary people and binary people (men and women).

The problem with living in a world so built upon binaries is that as soon as a new identity—or way of understanding ourselves—emerges, it quickly becomes defined in opposition to the thing that it's not. That's even clear in the umbrella term that we use "non-binary"—not binary gender.

So bisexuality becomes defined in opposition to monosexuality (see Chapter 1), non-monogamy in opposition to monogamy (see Chapter 3), and non-binary gender in opposition to binary gender.

But all of these binary opposites are problematic, first because it's hard—if not impossible—to draw clear lines between the two groups. With the bisexual/monosexual distinction, where do we put the man who identifies as straight but occasionally masturbates with another guy? Where do we put the gay person who is occasionally attracted to a celebrity of a different gender? Some people reach for outness as a way through the complexity. The only people who count as bi are the people who are out as bi. But that obscures all the many intersecting privileges and oppressions which make it far easier and safer for some people to be out than others.

With non-binary gender, given that we know that—even within a very binary culture—over a third of people will acknowledge feeling to some extent "the other gender, neither gender, or both genders", again we cannot simply draw a line around people who *identify* as non-binary. As we saw with the trans/cis binary in the previous section, such lines quickly lead to a whole set of judgments and assumptions about who is *really* non-binary and who isn't. This can make it very difficult, for example, for somebody whose only safe outlet feels like experimenting with "crossdressing" in a sexual context, and gets told that they aren't properly non-binary, even though that could—for them—be the first step on a journey towards a non-binary gender.

Also, as we've seen, the rules about who "counts" in each identity group easily take on many of the axes of oppression that exist in the wider culture—despite the group opposing social norms in respect to this one axis (in this case gender). So we see, for example, how the visible face of non-binary gender tends to be young, white, slim, masculine-of-centre or androgynous, educated middle class, and not disabled. The identity is therefore more difficult—or unwanted—to claim, the more a person sits outside of this privileged group. Some people might also feel that presenting as non-binary more visibly is simply not a safe option for them.

The drawing a line/not drawing a line binary

Is it as simple then as deciding simply not to draw a line? Anybody who wants to gets to say what they are: non-binary, or bisexual, or trans. Here we hit yet another unhelpful binary. Stay with us, it makes our heads spin too!

If we create a new binary between drawing lines around certain identities, and not doing so, and then say that the latter is better than the former, then we can also create problems. One is that, in a world which maps good/bad, right/wrong, and normal/abnormal binaries onto pretty much every identity and way of being, certain groups become far more marginalized and discriminated against than others.

When you spend much of your life under attack, or invisible, or both, it can be extremely valuable to create some spaces where you're around people with similar experiences, and can relax and get some support. This is why it can be really important to have women-only spaces, online communities for people of color, Pride events for LGBTQ+ folks, dating apps just for bis, and non-binary safer spaces at an event. But whenever such spaces emerge, there are controversies over who gets to use them and who doesn't. Much of this tends to come from more privileged people, for whom such spaces are a painful reminder of how we're all implicated in a system which marginalizes people. We can probably all remember times when we felt uncomfortable about the necessity for a safer space, and for many of us the kneejerk reaction is, unfortunately, to deny that need. However, there are also generally quite reasonable criticisms of such spaces around who actually gets to attend, given the trouble with drawing clear lines around any of those identities, and the long and painful histories of exclusion, for example of trans women from women-only spaces, and bi people from LGB communities.

Safer spaces are one area where we have to resist the urge to polarize into a good/bad binary, and hold the inevitable tensions around the fact that they can both include *and* exclude, they can both help people hugely *and* hurt people. We'll come back to this—and how hard it is—in the next chapter.

Another complexity of going towards the "not-drawing-lines" side of the binary is that there are real differences between the everyday lives of different people who might claim inclusion into a bi, or non-binary, community. For example, a woman who is married to a man but occasionally snogs a woman on a night out and doesn't mention it *does* have a different experience of bisexuality to a person who is out about being bi at work, and has partners of more than one gender. A person who is visibly gender non-conforming and requests gender neutral facilities has a very different experience of walking through the world to one who looks conventionally gendered and accepts using the expected toilets, changing rooms, and so on.

However, again we need to be careful, when it comes to individuals, not to make binary assumptions about who has the easier/more difficult time. It may be that the seemingly "bi-curious" woman in our first example simply couldn't be openly bi in her family or workplace due to the loss of community and sexual harassment she'd experience if she was. Possibly she is deeply unhappy in her marriage, and hates keeping secret this aspect of her life, which feels like a vital part of who she is. Perhaps our conventionally gendered person finds it excruciating that, whatever they did, nobody in our current world would ever read a body like theirs as attractively androgynous, and each time they "pass" in gendered spaces is a painful reminder of that.

Again we're going to have to hold the tension here between drawing lines to recognize those who are most oppressed by these cultural binaries (gay/straight, woman/man, etc.), and not drawing them in order to acknowledge that there are many who sit somewhere in between the binary, or who might appear to be on the more "normative" side of the binary when their experience is more on the "marginalized" side, or might be at some future date if they were allowed to explore that.

Problems with relating to the gender binary

A final problem with the binary/non-binary binary is that it still relates to the cultural gender binary (between men and women, or masculinity and femininity). It's about whether you feel like you fit into that binary, or whether you don't.

The problem here is that, as we've seen, the cultural gender binary is deeply problematic in itself. So what does it even mean to either locate yourself within it, or outside of it, as non-binary people do: either being *between* the man/woman binary, having aspects of *both*, or being *beyond* them in some third or further place?

> *Thought experiment: Which gender binary?*
> *To demonstrate this, try making a list of all the binaries that your wider culture tends to associate with the man/woman binary. For example, in the UK and US people tend to map this onto other binaries like rational/emotional, dominant/submissive, and independent/dependent. So masculinity is associated with the former in each case, and femininity with the latter. Come up with as many other examples as you can think of.*

Whether we look into our biology and psychology, or out into the world across time and culture, we can see that none of these things are intrinsically related to our gender. There's evidence—for all of these areas—of women who are more on the "male" side, and vice versa, and of whole communities and cultures where that is the case. And when psychological studies are done bringing all the previous research together, they find few consistent gender differences in any of these areas. Those that exist are are very small and may well be based on how different genders are taught to be in a particular society.

> ### Reflection point: Who fits which binary?
> Think about yourself, the people in your life, perhaps famous people you're aware of. If you created a spectrum out of each of the binaries you listed, can you think of a man or woman who is more on the other end of that spectrum than convention would expect? Are you, yourself, more on the expected end of each of those spectrums?

So if the gender binary itself is actually a long list of intersecting binaries, all of which are probably more usefully regarded as spectrums than binaries, what does it even mean to be non-binary? Is a non-binary person somebody who is in the middle of all those spectrums? Or somebody who is at the more "masculine" end on some, and the more "feminine" end on others? Depending on what we meant by gender at a particular time perhaps a person would shift from being binary to non-binary. For example you might be binary on rational/emotional, if you were assigned male at birth and acted more rationally than emotionally in general, but you might be non-binary on dominant/submissive, if you found that you had aspects of both of those traits in your character, or behaved more dominantly in some situations and more submisssively in others.

This easily begins to sound like the common criticism of anybody who identifies as non-binary: if gender is a social construct, which can be easily *deconstructed* in this way, then why make this stand about being non-binary instead of staying where you are—as a man or a woman—and critiquing the crappy hierarchical gender system?

One response to this is that given cultural gender norms are socially constructed, then the same criticism could be levelled at anybody who claims any gender identity. There's no reason to critique non-binary people for upholding the gender system any *more* than there is men or women. It's similar to the way that trans people who conform to gender norms—or who deviate from them—are often criticized way more than cis people who do so.

You can't step outside of culture

Also, vitally, as gender scholar Ros Gill points out, you can never step completely outside of culture. We can recognize the flaws in the gender system: how it is rooted in problematic hierarchical binaries, and means many different things at the same time, none of which are based in either biological or cultural universals. At the same time we grew up under that system and it is all around us all of the time. That means that all of us have to locate ourselves in some way in relation to that system. If we don't we risk being completely unintelligible to the people around us, and to ourselves, in ways would make everyday life difficult, if not impossible.

Just think about how hard it has been when people have endeavoured to locate themselves outside of the cultural gay/straight and man/woman binaries. When diver Tom Daley came out explicitly saying that he was attracted to men and women, without labelling himself, the mainstream media quickly imposed the label "gay" on him and the majority of people on social media refused to acknowledge his attraction to women as real. When non-binary folk like Fox Fisher and Owl, or Travis Alabanza, appear on TV or in the press the focus tends to be on pushing them back into a "male" or "female" box.

It's a hell of a lot to ask anybody to step outside of our current cultural way of viewing gender and sexuality completely. What would that even look like? The best we can do for now is to locate ourselves in relation to it in the way that feels most comfortable and consensual for us. We also have to acknowledge the complex feelings that we, no doubt, have around sexuality and gender, given that many of the cultural scripts that we've either accepted, or resisted, probably come with pleasures and joys for us, as well as limits and constraints. For example, at the same time as we criticize restrictive body ideals for women, we may delight in seeing a "feminine curve" on our own body or the body of another. At the same time as decrying toxic masculinity, we may feel pleasure when we find ourselves able to embody "masculine" power and strength and assert ourselves over another.

Perhaps all we can do for now is to acknowledge these complexities, and hold these tensions. Over the following chapters we'll think a lot more about how we can do this, particularly in relation to valuing and respecting our own experience—and the experience of others—at the same time as being critical of the cultural systems, structures, and scripts that constrain and oppress us.

Further Resources

You can read more about the gender binary, and non-binary gender, in the following books:

- Barker, M-J. and Scheele, J. (2019) *Gender: A Graphic Guide.* London: Icon Books.
- Barker, M-J. and Scheele, J. (2016) *Queer: A Graphic History.* London: Icon Books.
- Lester, CN (2017) *Trans Like Me.* London: Virago.

To apply these ideas more to your own gender, check these out:

- Alex's Ignite talk on Gender Liberation (youtube.com/watch?v=wWa77NCsksw)
- Alex's podcast Gender Stories (genderstories.buzzsprout.com)
- Bornstein, K. (2013) *My New Gender Workbook: A Step-by-Step Guide to Achieving World Peace through Gender Anarchy and Sex Positivity.* London: Routledge.
- Iantaffi, A. and Barker, M-J. (2017) *How to Understand Your Gender: A Practical Guide for Exploring Who You Are.* London: Jessica Kingsley Publishers. (rewriting-the-rules.com/zines—gender zine)

If you want to know more about gender, these website are great:

- Gender Construction Kit (genderkit.org.uk)
- Gendered Intelligence (genderedintelligence.co.uk)

CHAPTER 3

Relationships

At this point in the book we part company with the kinds of topics that you're likely to have heard discussed in relation to binaries before. There's generally at least some awareness that sexuality and gender are culturally assumed to be binary, whether or not people agree that this should be the case. However, we're usually far less familiar with applying non-binary approaches to topics like relationships, identities, bodies, emotions, and thinking. We don't tend to challenge binary thinking as much in these areas, or the inevitable hierarchies that are inherent in it: the notion that one side of the binary is somehow "better" or more "normal" than the other.

This chapter begins by exploring whether love—like sex and gender—could be seen as being structured by binaries. Starting with what are commonly considered our most intimate love relationships—romantic and sexual partnerships—we can see that these are certainly subject to binary understandings, particularly around whether we are in one or not. The "together/single" binary exerts a strong cultural pressure for people to form love relationships and to remain in them.

Another key binary here—which is often so taken for granted that it remains unexamined—is the monogamy/non-monogamy binary, where monogamous relationships are generally valued more highly—and seen as more "real" and serious—than non-monogamous ones. Along with the challenges posed to this by openly non-monogamous people, we explore the valuable questions that asexual and aromantic people have asked about the ways in which romantic and sexual relationships are prioritized over other kinds, and the ways that love and sex are assumed to naturally and normally come together in the same relationships.

Following from this it becomes clear that a major binary that structures love and relationships is the binary between romantic/sexual relationships and all other kinds. In the second section of the chapter we explore the binaries that people tend to draw between partners and friends, prioritizing the former over the latter. What happens to our understandings of love and relationships if we challenge this binary and consider treating lovers more like friends and friends more like lovers? What other kinds of love and relationships might we consider prioritizing?

This leads to the binary that we tend to draw between ourselves and others—which underlies all of our relationships. What happens when we start to question this divide: valuing ourselves and others equally, or even questioning whether we can distinguish our self from other beings? What happens when we ask ourselves what we mean when we divide the world into them and us, especially in conflict? We consider this not just from an individual but also a collective perspective. Finally, we consider the idea of intimacy and what can happen when we open up to the possibility of valuing multiple relationships. That's quite a lot to cover so let's begin!

3.1 Binaries in our intimate relationships

Together/single

One major binary in relationships divides couples from single people. The state of coupledom or togetherness is generally presented as far superior to singledom or soloness. We see this in the assumption that single folks must be dating or in search of a partner, and in the desperate fear that many people have of "ending up alone".

This is a staple of classic romantic comedies like *Sleepless in Seattle* where women are told they're more likely to be killed by a terrorist than to find a man to marry once they're over 40, and *Bridget Jones's Diary* where the main character is shown singing "All By Myself", drinking wine and wearing "unattractive" underpants as the cautionary tale of singledom. The many delights of solo living are seldom shown in the media, just as the pain, vulnerability, and often conflict of living alongside the same person for years and years are rarely depicted, unless a "break-up" is involved. What is the impact of seeing the repetition, over and over and over again, of the "happily-ever-after" of getting together with a partner as the ending of every story from fairy tale to action movie? How much do we internalize the notion that this is the goal we should be striving for?

The creation of a cultural bogeyman around singledom does a lot more damage than just to those who remain single. Like many of the binaries we're exploring, it also harms those on the more privileged or prioritized side of the binary. In this case those who are in relationships may well feel unable to leave them, because of the stigma attached to being single. This can lead to people staying in unfulfilling—and at worst abusive—relationships, and it can put a great deal of pressure on relationships, which can make them more likely to end. When relationships do break down, it can seriously exacerbate the suffering around breaking-up as the person is not just grieving the end of the relationship, but also struggling with shifting to the "bad" side of the together/single binary. It can also obscure the possibilities for retaining relationships with "exes" beyond the "staying together/breaking up" binary.

As with the sexuality and gender binaries, the together/single binary obscures all the relationship possibilities that are available between and beyond singledom and coupledom. For example solo poly people have multiple relationships from the place of being an independent unit, and there are also many living apart together couples (LATs) who find that this works very well for them, as well as those who live as part of more communal homes or extended families. Expanding this binary would give us much more scope for finding the relationship with ourselves and with others that works best for us, at any given point in time.

Monogamous/non-monogamous

Another relationship binary that we've written about a lot is the monogamy/non-monogamy binary. Again this tends to privilege the former over the latter, despite the fact that non-monogamous relationships are actually more common globally than monogamous ones—in terms of the number of communities practicing them. Also a significant minority—or possibly even majority—of supposedly monogamous relationships in Western dominant cultures are secretly—and often unethically—non-monogamous at least at some point.

The prioritizing of the monogamous love side of the binary is extremely strong. Think about all the media depictions of somebody being attracted to more than one person at once. In virtually every case that individual is presented as having to make a choice between the two people they have feelings for, beginning in young adult fiction like *Twilight* and *The Hunger Games*.

87

Therefore it can be very hard for those who try to step outside of monogamy to live an openly non-monogamous life. There are no legal rights or protections available to them, and a good deal of cultural stigma to face.

Again this way of thinking obscures the wide diversity of ways of doing relationships which blur and break the binary. For example monogamish relationships are somewhat open. Soft swinging involves people having physical or flirtatious encounters with others which stop short of sex. There are people in couples who stay close with their exes, who have a rich life of online sex with other people, or who hold a 50-mile rule that enables them to have sexual encounters when they're away from home. Again moving away from the binary enables people to find a relationship style and structure that works for them.

> **Thought experiment: Spectrums of monogamy**
> *We've seen throughout the book how it can be useful to shift binaries by replacing them with spectrums. Try locating yourself on the following spectrums of monogamy. Are there still limitations in representing non/monogamy in this way?*
>
> SPECTRUM OF EMOTIONAL CLOSENESS
> **Monoamorous** ---------------------------------- **Polyamorous**
> One emotionally close   Multiple
> relationship, no close   emotionally close
> relationships beyond this   relationships
>
> SPECTRUM OF PHYSICAL CONTACT
> **Monosexual** ------------------------------------- **Polysexual**
> One sexual relationship,   Multiple sexual
> no sex/physical contact   relationships/
> beyond this   encounters

The monogamy/non-monogamy binary presents us with a useful example of why it's not helpful simply to flip the binary. In some writing about non-monogamous relationships, writers have endeavored to present them as more natural, normal, and better than monogamous ones, for example by reporting on how most animal species are non-monogamous, or by presenting non-monogamy as inherently more ethical than monogamy. Not only does this risk monogamous people feeling excluded in communities where this flipped hierarchy becomes the norm, it also prevents us from thinking critically about the forms of non-monogamy that predominate. In recent years polyamorous and open communities have been challenged to consider the further exclusions and norms that have developed there, for example around "unicorn hunting" to find the perfect person to complete a triad, or insistences that new partners join a polycule or practice non-monogamy in a particular way. They've also been critiqued for failing to question other cultural binaries beyond monogamy/non-monogamy, such as those which privilege white, middle-class people; the gender binary; and binaries of love relationships over other kinds.

Romantic/sexual

Across monogamous relationships, non-monogamous relationships, and those in between, another binary often remains in place which privileges romantic relationships over purely sexual ones. It's this approach which positions polyamory as "superior" to swinging, for example, or which looks down on "casual" sex encounters and stigmatizes sex workers and their clients. This binary often results in more sex-focused relationships being treated as disposable: ditched by monogamous people when a romantic relationship comes along, or objectified as "secondary" in non-monogamous communities.

Asexual (ace) and aromantic (aro) people have usefully challenged the assumption underlying this binary: that it's best to get romantic and sexual needs and desires met in the same relationship—and that it's even necessary to have such needs. Many asexual people form close relationships which are not sexual—but which may or may not be romantic; and many aromantic people form close relationships which are not romantic—but which may or may not be sexual. Consider the diversity of ways relating in the following list:

Multiple experiences: Diversities of asexual, sexual, aromantic, and romantic ways of relating

- "I'm ace. For me that means I don't experience sexual attraction. I have a romantic partner and we express our love with cuddles and sweet words and sleeping together, just never sexually."
- "As an aromantic person I don't experience romantic attraction at all. I totally have sexual attractions though, and it can be difficult to get sexual partners to understand that just because I'm sexual with them does not mean we'll ever have a romantic relationship, or move in together, or any of that stuff."
- "I'm demisexual which means that I only ever experience sexual attraction with people I'm already strongly emotionally connected with. I'm also polyamorous so I currently have two people I do have sex with: one's a partner and the other is a really close friend. I'm mostly homoromantic so both those people are the same gender as me."
- "I'd say I was gray A: somewhere between asexual and allosexual. I do have flickers of sexual attraction, but

it's not common for me, and I can have long stretches without any. Generally I prefer solo sex to sex with other people."

- "I'm into building queerplatonic relationships: these are really close bonds with other queer people which don't buy into cultural ideals about romantic relationships. Like we wouldn't see ourselves as belonging to each other but we do make strong commitments, and what we see as romantic doesn't look much like the Valentine's Day version!"

This helps us to begin to question the assumption that our most important relationships are *necessarily* the romantic/sexual ones, as well as the assumption that we should be getting all these things (romance, sex, closeness, etc.) in the same relationship. We'll explore this more in the next section.

3.2 Partners/friends and self/other

Partner/friend

Perhaps an overarching binary when it comes to love and relationships is the one which privileges partners over friends. You can see this reflected in phrases like "just friends", "more than friends" and "friendzone", all of which suggest that being friends is inferior to—and less desirable than—being partners with someone. This kind of thinking means we can often neglect our friends when embarking on a new relationship and expect to be forgiven for it. Also notice how the word "relationship" in the previous sentence fails to include the very real relationships we have with our friends.

Along with the binaries we explored in the previous section, the partner/friend binary places coupled, monogamous, romantic, sexual, partnered love right at the pinnacle of human experience. Like the sexual and gender binaries this is quite a new, Western dominant culture thing to do, and certainly not the way that relationships have been done globally, or across time. In recent years, relationship anarchists, in particular, have presented important challenges to this model of placing one romantic relationship above all others.

This kind of binary hierarchy puts one love relationship under a huge amount of pressure to fulfil all of our—often contradictory—needs and desires. This often leads to people leaving each relationship quickly because it can never meet their expectations, resulting in them being bruised by multiple break-ups. On the flip side, it also often results in people remaining stuck in relationships that are bad for them because of the pressure to have a partner, and because challenging any or all of these binaries is so unthinkable.

The answer is not to replace one kind of love with another as the pinnacle of human relationships. For example, there have been some shifts in recent years to replace the relationship between partners with the relationship between parent and child at the top of the hierarchy as a truer, more enduring and unconditional, kind of love. Just like partner relationships, this risks us de-emphasizing other important relationships in our lives, and putting too much pressure on parent-child relationships. For example, children may feel that they have to live out their parents dreams for them, or parents may feel that their whole identities must be bound up in their parenthood. There would be similar issues if, for example, we put a polyamorous cluster or polycule at the top of a hierarchy, or a best friend relationship, or a working partnership. Basically a hierarchical approach simply does not seem to work so well in relationships.

A useful way of challenging this binary, hierarchical approach to love entirely goes back to the Ancient Greeks. They came up with seven different kinds of love which we might want to ensure that we make space for in our lives, shown in Figure 3.1. You might realize, looking at it, that we already need to expand these seven to at least eight given what we learnt from aromantic and asexual folk about how romantic and sexual relationships can be separate as well as combined.

Figure 3.1: Ancient Greek words for love

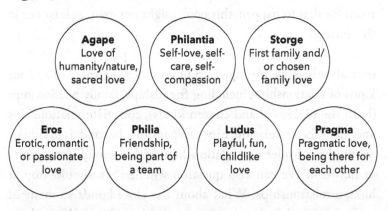

Thought experiment: Different kinds of love
Think about these different kinds of love. Would you want to add any more? Or remove any that don't feel are relevant to you? Once you have a list that works for you, consider whether—and where—you experience these kinds of love in your own life. Are there kinds of love you'd like to emphasize more, or prioritize less?

Expanding out the different kinds of love in this way can help us to recognize the importance of diverse kinds of relationships in our lives. This is something that's very important for us—your authors—given the close relationship we have with each other. We both feel that our relationship is just as important as some of the sexual and romantic relationships in our lives. There is an intimacy that comes with writing together and getting excited about ideas which is unique and just as valuable as, for example, having sex together and getting excited about each other's bodies. Also creating something together which neither of us could possibly have created alone, and then sharing that with others, is an extremely powerful experience. We also want to acknowledge how our relationship shifted and changed in the decade and a half we've known each other. If we had not given room for that to happen, this book might not exist, at least not in this format!

Once we question the prioritization of partner relationships over all others we can open up to consider the value of various kinds of relationships, including friendships, family relationships (both the biological and chosen kinds), collegiate relationships, and neighbour relationships. Expanding beyond individuals we might consider our relationships with a group, community, or network. We can also question whether we should stop at human relationships. What about the close bonds so many of us form with the companion animals in our lives? What about our relationships to certain places, or objects, or projects? And how about considering our relationships with nature, with the planet, with the spirit or divinity, or with the ecosystem around us? We'll come back to some of these themes in the rest of the chapter.

The self/other binary

Binary ways of doing relationships tend to exacerbate another binary: the binary between ourselves and another person, such as a partner. Black feminist writer bell hooks and others have pointed out that love is simply not possible in a relationship where the self is valued far more highly than the other, or vice versa. What we have under these conditions is the tendency to treat the other person as a thing for our own benefit, and to try to make them into what we want them to be. Or we have the tendency to treat ourselves as a thing for somebody else and to try to shape ourselves into their ideal.

Reflection point: Self and other

Think about this in your own relationships. Are there times when you value yourself over the other person; are there times when you value yourself over them? What happens when you do one or the other? You might want to consider relationship conflicts in particular. What would it look like to value yourself and the other person equally at such times?

All of the following things flow from the interconnected cultural love binaries we've covered in the chapter so far:

- the privileging of being in a couple over being with ourselves
- the notion of belonging to someone else
- the assumption that we will let go of our friends and support networks and keep "the relationship" private from them
- the expectation that we will squash down many of our needs and desires for the sake of "the relationship" and perhaps force ourselves to match up to the relationship ideal, for example by having sex of a certain type and frequency, even if we don't want it.

It's here that the concept of decolonial love can also be helpful. It locates our current binary ways of loving in the stream of histories of settler colonialism and slavery, which involved treating other people as things for our own benefit. It imagines other forms of love where we value ourselves and others equally. This includes imagining love with consent and care for self and other at its heart, where a critical reflection on power dynamics is ongoing, and where there is a commitment to never treat another person—or yourself—as property that somebody is entitled to in terms of a particular kind of relationship, or form of labour that is expected.

This type of love is rooted in interdependence, which, by its nature, does not lend itself easily to hierarchies. Critical disability studies and Indigenous studies, alongside Black feminist scholarship, have highlighted how the independent/dependent binary is unhelpful and incorrect, given that we are interdependent. Interdependence reminds us that we are connected, not just to other humans but also to the broader ecosystem. Many spiritual traditions, such as Buddhism, also challenge the idea of separation—or even the existence—of the individualized self. In the next section, we go back to discussing the us/them and insider/outsider binaries in a little more depth.

Slow down!

This seems like a good time to take a moment to yourself.

Take a few breaths and maybe even go back to the slow down page in the first chapter, where you were invited to breathe into contact and support. Once you feel as grounded and present as you can be in this moment, notice what you may want to do or not do right now. For example, do you want to carry on reading, or not? Do you need to have a stretch break, or go to the bathroom, or have a drink of water?

Too often, as we struggle with balancing our needs with other people's needs, we end up overriding ourselves. This means that we might cross our own boundaries.

This slow down page is all about self-consent. What do you want to say "yes", "no", or "maybe later" to in this moment? Where does that yes, no or maybe live in your body? How do you know what you want and don't want? Don't worry if you feel you cannot do this. It's okay. Sometimes it takes asking ourselves "what do I want?" a few times before we find our answers.

Many of us were brought up to not pay close attention to our needs, to neglect them, or to only meet them after other people's needs were met first.

Whatever you said yes, no or maybe to, we hope you keep practicing self-consent as much as you can.

Do you want to carry on reading right now? If so, that's great. If not, don't worry, you can always come back to this book later, when you want to.

3.3 Looking at the foundations of human relationships

Many models of psychological development in Western dominant culture do include the idea of self/other through concepts such as individuation; that is the way that something is different from something else. For example, sometimes therapists talk about adolescents individuating from their parents, as in becoming distinct and different from them. It can, at times, seem that the idea of self/other is unavoidable and maybe even "natural". When the binary self/other is then applied to a group of people, the leap to us/them seems logical and, once again, maybe "natural". The us can be our family of origin, an identity group to whom we feel a sense of belonging, a nation, or a religion, for example.

Us/them: a matter of survival?
Dividing the world into us/them makes sense on some level. After all knowing who is "with us" and who is not can be essential to our survival. This is poignantly depicted in the series of young adult novels and movies *The Hunger Games*. In this dystopian future, a whole system of hierarchical power is upheld by setting people against one another in a celebration of personal survival as collective strength for the district they represent. The only people who are not directly involved are the bystanders who live in the Capitol, who are set also as "other" through their separation from participating in the games.

We won't give any more spoilers about what happens in this particular world, but we would like to discuss what happens in *our* world when we, similarly, start to believe there is always an us/them divide. This divide is essentially at the heart of every conflict and war. Genocide of Indigenous populations globally was and is possible because there's a framing of these populations as "different" and "lesser than" from the people who want to take over the land on which they live. The survival of settler colonial groups is seen as more important than theirs. Historically othering and dividing people into us/them has been achieved through many categories: wealth, class, land ownership, religion, skin color, and more.

But whose survival matters and who decides this? For many of us, in Western dominant cultures, corporations and governments would have us believe that our survival might depend on access to oil and other natural resources. However, when we understand that we are interdependent not only from one another, but also from our relationship to the Earth, we might consider other perspectives. We might start to think about the survival of generations to come, as many Indigenous people already do, not only for human animal generations but also green bloods, such as plants, trees, vegetations, and wetlands. We might also start to pay more attention to the difference between survival and preservation of our way of life, given that the two are not the same thing.

Along with the destruction of people and nations—and their legacies—another deep wound of settler colonialism and slavery is the us/them binary of humans/nature. This tells us that we don't belong with other mammals, teaching us that we're not interdependent with every other species in the global ecosystem, and that the land is something we can own. Once that wound is inflicted, it becomes increasingly easy to separate people from other people. As we have become a more global society, it has become easier still to separate us on other bases such as nationalities, class, race, and other aspects of identity and experience.

When we divide the world into us/them though, we do not only start to dehumanize the other, as we can see in every form of slavery and genocide. We begin to also dehumanize ourselves. If we start to think that we can own the land, green bloods and red bloods—that is animals—then we can also own people, if we can categorize them as not fully human in some ways. There is already comprehensive scholarship on these topics, so we won't discuss this much further here (see the Further Resources section at the end of this chapter). However, we wanted to make sure we included this to illustrate just how damaging binary thinking can be to human relationships, and how foundational to much of dominant culture it is.

Before moving onto the next section on insider/outsider, let's unpack what we mean by dehumanizing ourselves a little more. If we can conceptualize other living things as objects and potential property in some ways, we're distancing from parts of ourselves. What separates us from them? How do we commodify ourselves? For example, we might separate mind and body, as we discuss later in Chapter 5. We might ask of our own selves more than we're capable of, because we start thinking of our body as a vessel, and not as being us. When we start to divide the world into us and them, we not only enter conflict with one another, we also enter into deep conflict with our own selves. We damage our relationships with ourselves, with the world around us, and with one another, both on micro and macro levels.

Thought experiment: How do we know who is "us" and who is "them"?

Take a moment to think and journal about your relationships, if you want. Who do you consider to be like you? Who do you consider to be different from you? Once you have listed all those that you feel are like you and those who are unlike you, take time to notice whether there are differences between the people who are like you, and also between the people who are not like you. Where does "us" become "them"? Where does "them" become "us"? Are there experiences and identities you might share with people in both lists? Are there experiences and identities that are different from people on both lists? Please remember that you do not need to like or understand in either list. This is simply an exercise in noticing similarities es so that we can reflect on how we decide who belongs

*with "us" and who belongs with "them". You may also want to notice
how this changes over time and how you might have felt like you
belonged with different people at different times in your life. We do
come back to the idea of changes over time in Chapter 4.*

Challenging insider/outsider perspectives

Once there is an us/them, another binary easily emerges: insider/
outsider. This often layers on the us/them binary so that "us" usually
equals insiders and "them" outsiders. Where the borders are, or
who is inside of them and who is outside, can of course be quite
a moveable feast, including over time. For example, we—MJ and
Alex—have been inside and outside of each other's inner circle of
close people more than once over the years, as our relationship
changed yet we remained in one another's lives.

Insider/outsider is a little different than us/them though. In
many ways, it can be more nuanced. We might be incredibly close
to someone and consider them part of "us"—our family, our people,
or our community. Then, something happens; maybe we have a
different experience, which puts them outside and us inside. For
example, we might be the first person in our group of close friends
to get pregnant, have a miscarriage, or an abortion. Suddenly our
friends who do not share that experience might be outside of it,
while people who were strangers yesterday might become part of
a close network of social support because they share that specific
experience with us.

The insider/outsider binary then seems much less stable than
us/them in many ways. "Us" implies a certain level of commitment
to one another and/or homogeneity, or at least some firmly shared
traits. Insider/outsider could be much more dependent on temporal
and circumstantial variables. Both binaries though raise questions
of who decides who is inside/outside and who is part of "us", as well
as begging the questions: inside/outside of what? And according
to which categories do we define us/them? Interestingly us/them

and insider/outsider seem to be two connected and interdependent binaries. To be part of an "us" we're usually inside certain criteria, and to be one of "them" we're usually outside of the criteria that define the "us", and maybe inside a different set of criteria.

Does all this sound incredibly confusing? Maybe it's because it is! As humans, we want to draw lines around noticeable differences and similarities, and the assumptions we make based on these. We are, after all, meaning-making people and we might also be trying to figure out who is "safe" for us to be around—something that has become increasingly difficult as we've become more and more disconnected from local communities. However, those assumptions may be right or wrong, or most likely all over the place. If we decide, without much information, that someone is outside of our circle based on appearance, or something they have said, we might find out that this is not the case. Of course sometimes our assumptions are correct. It seems that when it comes to us/them and insider/outsider we rely an awful lot on probability, and all too often end up mistaking it for certainty. Let's unpack this a little more.

We might be relying on applying current social clues on someone's historical accumulation of experiences. For example, we might make assumptions about someone's class upbringing based on their current socioeconomic status and education. We're reading the correct and current social clues but we're applying them to that person historically without really knowing them. This means we might consider someone who is currently educated and in a middle-class position in life to be categorically outside of working-class experience, even when they have been brought up working class.

We might, at times, also be applying one categorical social lens to an individual who is much more than a singular aspect of their identities. For example, if someone talks about their Christian faith, and the depth of their devotion, we might make an assumption that they might be cisgender and straight, and maybe even transphobic and queerphobic, given that there is such a frequent and dominant narrative of Christianity as rejecting of trans and queer people. However, there are many trans and queer people who belong to a broad range of faiths and religions, including Christianity, and who might be part of inclusive congregations.

On the other hand, if we reduce everything to the individual, we might risk being unaware of larger social issues, which might benefit an entire group of people. For example, when people complain of toxic masculinity, its traits and behaviors, many men might feel this is an individual attack on them and retreat into a "not all men" position instead of really listening to what's being expressed.

We cannot reduce everything to a purely individual level because we are indeed inside and outside of historical, cultural, and social systems, whether we like it or not. If we reduce everything to the personal, we no longer understand the systemic power, privilege, and oppression operating in the world, and think that everything is possible for everybody, and that everyone is equal already! Sadly we know that too many people are far from equal in our world and that none of us can be free until we're all free—to paraphrase Emma Lazarus.[1] We return to this in Chapter 4 when we address issues such as which bodies matter and which don't in dominant culture.

As with many binaries, us/them and insider/outsider can in fact be useful lenses that are heavily dependent on our discernment and flexibility. Like we said, we're inside and outside of certain social, cultural, and historical categories, whether we like it or not. Many of us also fall in between categories, of course, living at their

---

1   This relates to the story behind the Statue of Liberty—see https://en.wikipedia.org/wiki/The_New_Colossus

borders, both physically and metaphorically, as we discuss more in Chapter 4 as well.

What would happen then if we were more intentional about noticing who us/them are and when we're the insider or the outsider, or both at once? And what would happen if we also paid attention to all the ways in which the status of insider/outsider can shift and change, even within the space of a conversation? Our hypothesis is that our relationships with ourselves, the world around us and one another might change and be impacted by our curiosity, attention, and care. There might be even more possibility for intimacy, as we discuss in the following section. Before moving on though, here are some experiences of people reflecting on the insider/outsider status in their lives.

Multiple experiences: Dancing inside, outside, and all around the edges in relationships

- "It took me a long time to notice that my now partner of 20 years was courting me. They were dating a lot of women at the time and hanging out at the lesbian bar. I was a cis straight man. I just assumed they wouldn't be into me. I made a lot of assumptions about their sexuality and, as it turned out later, their gender and my own sexuality. If a friend hadn't spelled it out for me, I would have missed out on an amazing relationship. Also, if I had been too attached to staying strictly inside the norms of heterosexuality, we might not have lasted. I'm glad I learned I could step outside for this."

- "For the longest time I just didn't come out to any Black co-workers. I had bought into the racist trope that Black people are homophobic. When one of them came out to me I felt so ashamed. Here they were, taking this tremendous risk, at a workplace that was predominantly white, not knowing whether I was safe or not, and I had been hiding inside my prejudice all that time while thinking of myself as a 'good, liberal person'."

- "When my child died by suicide I just felt outside my own life. Nothing made sense anymore. Nobody made sense anymore. Other parents couldn't even look at me. I was their worst fear. Or maybe they thought I could do more. I don't know. All I know is that I was definitely no longer one of them. I was a single parent so I didn't even have a partner who was going through this with me. It was only when I met other parents whose children had died by suicide that I felt understood again. I was no longer completely alone. That helped. I had to find a way back, for the sake of my other children."

- "I left the clergy in my 50s. I had entered the seminary when I was in my 20s. That is a long time to be part of something and then, suddenly, not even be allowed to take communion anymore because I had come out as gay. All of the sudden I wasn't just outside of my religion but I had also lost my home, my community, my friends, and I almost lost my faith. Eventually I found an inclusive congregation in a different Christian denomination. That was helpful. I could come back to myself a little more. I didn't need to leave any part of me out in the cold so that I could belong somewhere."

- "The only people who can spot I'm disabled are usually other people with chronic health issues. They notice how I might get up from a chair, walk, or breathe through my shirt when an intense smell enters the room. There is some comfort in feeling seen, in not being invisible, in not having someone walk confidently towards the stairs while you tag along because you don't have the spoons to explain you need to take the elevator."

3.4 The possibility of multiple intimacies

The binary of insider/outsider can create its own kind of immediate intimacy when we share powerful experiences with others. For example, in 2006 Black activist Tarana Burke started the hashtag #MeToo, which was picked up a decade later by several people, including white celebrities, to illustrate just how widespread sexual violence against women and femmes is. Many women and survivors of all genders felt they could finally speak out and be part of something greater than themselves. The hashtag became a movement they could be inside of. However, other women and survivors of sexual violence of all genders also found the hashtag to be triggering.

All of the sudden social media feeds did indeed show how widespread misogynistic sexual violence truly is. This was challenging for many survivors and empowering for others. Some survivors were ready to—and wanted to—share their stories out loud. Other survivors were muting their feed so they could still be on social media, as one of their networks of support, but not feel constantly triggered. To trouble the issue further, male and non-binary survivors were not sure if they could use the hashtag, and some were even berated for doing so because this was not "their movement", even though they had also been subject to the same sexual violence rooted in patriarchy. Who was inside or outside of the movement? Who did the movement belong to?

Many Black women also felt alienated since they knew the hashtag had been started by a Black woman, but now white celebrities were garnering all the attention. Some felt that the increased attention was due to the fact that sexual violence against white women is seen as unacceptable whereas violence against Black women is seen as the norm. Suddenly, some Black women who had been at the beginning of the movement felt the movement had been co-opted and appropriated by people—white women—who also participated in perpetrating systemic violence against them.

Yes, this is all very complicated. There are no right or wrong answers necessarily in this complex web. At its heart, there is a desire to not be alone, to belong, to be inside of something: a movement, a group with shared identities, an experience of pain and healing. All the people involved in this messy situation were survivors of sexual violence. Many were also subject to systemic racial violence, while others were not. The racial violence was also inextricably linked with the sexual violence many had experienced, because their bodies were sexualized in certain ways due to being racialized in certain ways.

The desire to be seen, to not be erased, to not be pushed out of the movement is also about wanting to heal together. We heal in community. Given that most trauma happens in the context of relationships, it is in the context of relationships that we might find the potential for healing. However, relationships are messy and complicated. They do not happen in a vacuum; they happen in larger and smaller systems, riddled with all the binaries we discuss in this entire book. The #MeToo movement was born, among other things, from a desire to connect and to find the intimacy of shared experience with other survivors.

Reflection point: The intimacy of shared experiences
Have there been times in your life when you sought out people who shared similar experiences to yours? If so—and if you found them—what difference did that make? If you have felt alone in some of your experiences, what was that like? When you're suffering, is it easier for you to be by yourself or with others who share a similar experience of suffering?

Many types of intimacy

What is intimacy though? We might think of intimacy as something that close romantic and/or sexual partners share. However, there are many types of intimacy. If intimacy is about closeness—and we believe it is—we can experience it in a range of relationships. For example, in Chapter 1 we discussed ecosexuality, and how many people find intimacy with nature to be erotic, or nurturing, or both. We can have intimacy with ourselves, with the world around us, and with others. How well do we know ourselves for example? Do we know our own boundaries: our yes, our no, and our maybe, which we invited you to notice in the slow down page earlier in this chapter?

Boundaries are important to intimacy because, to experience closeness, we also need to feel a sense of trust so that we can relax into it. Once we know we can trust someone, we can relax into the closeness of sharing an experience with them. We talk more about what we mean by experience a little later in this section, and how the types of experiences we share might define different types of intimacies. Knowing our yes, no, and maybe, and generally being close with our own selves can only happen in the context of decolonial love. If we can value ourselves and others equally, if we do not think we have the right to somebody else's yes, and do not expect them to have the right to ours, then we can trust both ourselves and others.

This can be rather counter-cultural given that it implies that we have sovereignty over our own selves and our own selves alone, in a dominant culture that tries to tell us that we have sovereignty over land or others. At the same time, dominant culture instills in us self-doubt, so that we can be sold things to help us feel better about ourselves. Knowing who we are, what we want, and being able to express our needs, wants, and desires—so that we can find others to share them with—makes us poor targets for capitalism, because we can now access intimacy in many ways, with several beings, and even by ourselves. This type of knowing is rooted in radical self-care, an acceptance of interdependence, and radical self-love (see Further Resources on these topics at the end of the chapter).

Basically when we're open to having a fully consensual relationship with ourselves and with others, and do not expect one person or a small nuclear family to meet all of our needs, the landscape of intimacy opens. What does it open up onto though? If intimacy means more than the closeness of a family unit, or a euphemism for sexual intercourse, what other types of intimacies are available to us? Let's look at some examples we might all be familiar with, but might not have previously thought of as part of intimacy.

Many of us might have joked about having a "work spouse/husband/wife" for example. This term is sometimes used to indicate the person who shares our day-to-day life at work. They might be the ones who know when we're having a tough time, or help us celebrate our victories. They are people we might choose to work more closely with. There is a work intimacy born out of sharing responsibilities. The people we live with, including partners and spouses, share work intimacy with us as well. With them we share the unpaid labor of raising a family, making meals, cleaning the house, and so on. Work intimacy is basically the closeness that can emerge from sharing labor—whether paid or unpaid—on a regular basis.

For many disabled people, there is also a specific type of intimacy, which Mia Mingus calls access intimacy. Access intimacy is not just for disabled people; it can also be experienced by many other people who might share experiences of marginalization, such as people of color or trans people. Mia describes access intimacy as "that elusive, hard to describe feeling when someone else "gets" your access needs. The kind of eerie comfort that your disabled self feels with someone on a purely access level."[2] Mia goes on to talk about how it can happen with people with whom there are long-lasting relationships and people we've just met. Mia describes access intimacy also as the closeness that emerges from "an automatic understanding of access needs out of our shared similar lived experience of the many different ways ableism manifests in our lives."[3]

Another form of intimacy is recreational intimacy. Who do we share leisure activities with? Who do we have fun with? Sharing favorite activities, such as watching a movie together, taking a walk, or playing sports also breeds closeness. This can be clearly seen in many sports teams both at times of victory and of loss, when people huddle together to celebrate or bemoan. As well as recreational intimacy, there is aesthetic intimacy, or—as Alex renamed it—delight intimacy. This is about who we share experiences of beauty with, such as watching a sunset, reading a poem, and so on. There is, of course, overlap between different types of intimacy, and we might experience more than one at the same time.

We share mind intimacy with those who we share ideas with. Who knows our opinions and favorite books or music? Who do we share our intellectual world with? Similarly, who do we share our emotional inner world with, leading to emotional intimacy? The list goes on, and it does indeed include emotional and sexual intimacies that are maybe the most well-known types of intimacy, and the most immediately thought of when discussing the topic.

---

2   See leavingevidence.wordpress.com/2011/05/05/access-intimacy-the-missing-link, accessed on 21 November 2018.

3   See leavingevidence.wordpress.com/2011/05/05/access-intimacy-the-missing-link, accessed on 21 November 2018.

Not all types of intimacy are equally important to different people. It's useful to know what types of intimacies are important to us and those around us. We do not need to have the same preferences, but it is helpful to understand where we converge and where we diverge from our loved ones when it comes to the types of closeness we're seeking through our relationships. In the thought experiment below, we have included several types of intimacy that have been identified by systemic and sex therapists. If you find types of intimacy we have not listed, please let us know, and feel free to add your own. We have so much more capacity for intimacy, connection, and relationships than we might think.

> ### Thought experiment: Assessing your intimacy needs
> *This is an opportunity to reflect on your intimacy needs: where they are met, where they are not, and how important they are to you. First of all, think about who meets the 13 aspects of intimacy listed over the page. This might involve one or more people for each aspect. Once you have done that, please indicate to which degree each of these aspects of intimacy is satisfied in your life.*
>
> *You can use a scale of 1 to 10 with 1 being not at all satisfied (needs are not met) to completely satisfied (all your needs in this aspect are met). You can also make up your own scale!*
>
> *Finally, rank each aspect in order of importance with 1 being the most important and 13 the least important. Remember that there is no right or wrong answer. This is your own assessment and it reflects your own values, experiences, and needs.*[4]

---

4   Please note that Alex adapted this exercise from existing materials by Clinebell and Clinebell (1970), Metz and Mia Mingus (leavingevidence. wordpress.com/2011/05/05/access-intimacy-the-missing-link).

Types of intimacy	Who meets these needs?	Current satisfaction	Rank of importance
Work sharing tasks, supporting each other in various responsibilities (e.g. raising family, house chores)			
Recreation sharing experiences of play (e.g. fun activities, sports, hobbies)			
Mind sharing the world of ideas (e.g. reading, discussing a movie)			
Commitment togetherness through dedication to common values/ideals (e.g. doing activism together)			
Delight sharing experiences of beauty (e.g. nature, art, dance, theatre, interior decor)			
Communication being truthful and open with each other (e.g. giving constructive feedback)			
Emotion sharing significant feelings (e.g. being vulnerable, emotionally open, and available)			
Creativity helping others to grow and celebrate them as co-creators (e.g. nurturing self-development, celebrating change)			

Access an implicit understanding of access needs out of shared similar lived experience of the many different ways oppression manifests in our lives (e.g. being able to be present with someone's trauma, immediately know that access needs are present and meeting them, such as grabbing a different type of seating)			
Sexual sharing sensual, physical, and sexual experiences (e.g. cuddling, kissing, having sex)			
Crisis experiencing closeness through standing together at painful/difficult times (e.g. death of a loved one, illness)			
Conflict facing differences, negotiating conflict resolution (e.g. arguing, disagreeing)			
Spirituality sharing a sense of communion/belonging (e.g. philosophical or religious experiences, the meanings of life)			

Further Resources

You can read more about the single/together, monogamy/non-monogamy, partner/friend, and staying-together/breaking-up binaries —and alternatives to these—in:

- Barker, M-J. (2018) *Rewriting the Rules: An Anti-Self-Help Guide to Love, Sex and Relationships*. London: Routledge.

There's also a zine that Meg-John wrote with Justin Hancock where you can explore more your own approach to relationships, beyond binaries:

- megjohnandjustin.com/product/make-your-own-relation ship-user-guide

bell hooks's writing on love is very helpful for considering how we tend to value ourselves and others in relationships:

- hooks, b. (2000) *All About Love: New Visions*. London: Harper Perennial.

Some similar ideas are explored, from a Buddhist perspective, in:

- Welwood, J. (2006) *Perfect Love, Imperfect Relationships*. Boston, MA: Trumpeter.

Consented magazine offers some wonderful anthologies of intersectional thinking around topics like gender and mental health. The issue on love and desire is excellent on the topics covered in this chapter:

- *Consented* (2018) *Love and Desire*. Available from: consented. bigcartel.com/product/issue-5-love-desire

Here are some other resources you might find useful:

- Barker, M-J. (2016) *Hell Yeah Self Care*. From rewriting-the-rules/zines
- Gwendolywn (Mitikomis) Benaway on decolonial love: workingitouttogether.com/content/decolonial-love-a-how-to-guide
- Joyful Militancy on friendship: joyfulmilitancy.com/2017/ 12/11/friendship-as-a-root-of-freedom
- Love Uncommon on Self Consent: loveuncommon. com/2017/09/28/self-consent
- Mia Mingus on access intimacy:
  - leavingevidence.wordpress.com/2011/05/05/access-intimacy-the-missing-link,
  - leavingevidence.wordpress.com/2017/04/12/access-intimacy-interdependence-and-disability-justice
- Taylor, S.R. (2018) *The Body is Not an Apology*. Oakland, CA: Berrett-Koehler Publishers.

CHAPTER 4

Bodies

When we're in relationship with others, as well as with ourselves and the land, we cannot help but be in our bodies to a certain degree. Even when we feel completely disembodied, as long as we're alive our hearts are beating and our breath is always there. We exist as bodies. We'll talk more about the mind/body binary in the next chapter. In this chapter we consider all the different binaries that dominant culture places on bodies and how we might have internalized those.

Bodies are defiant of binaries, both individually and collectively. We hold multitudes of identities, experiences, and even time, within our bodies. For example, our bodies hold different experiences of power, privilege and oppression. Our bodies know both/and already, even as our thoughts might struggle with holding paradox. We hold complexities within ourselves that we then try to untangle through thinking and language: complexities that simply are.

We discuss some of these complexities in this chapter: from

experiences of existing across geographical, social, cultural, racial, and class borders, to the idea of fluidity across time, and exploring the idea of time itself. We then address the disabled/abled and ill/healthy binaries as well as many of the other ways in which dominant culture has tried to split and "other" our bodies to the point that some bodies matter more than others in existing systems.

4.1 Further non-binary identities and experiences

As we've seen in previous chapters, when people consider non-binary identities or experiences they're likely to think of bisexuality, and—these days—they might also think of non-binary genders. However, there are people with non-binary experiences in all of the different categories that are used to capture people's identities, bodies, and histories, such as race, culture, class, faith, disability, and age.

In this section we consider experiences that are between binaries, both/and or mixed, and beyond binaries. In the next section we'll look at ones that vary over the course of people's lives—in a similar way to sexual or gender fluidity, and relationships over time (see Chapters 1, 2, and 3).

Let's start with our own personal experiences of other non-binary aspects of ourselves so you can see the kind of things we're talking about.

Alex writes...

Growing up in Italy I was aware pretty early on of the North/South divide in my country. My mom is from Sicily and we spent all of our holidays there growing up. She also has darker skin and my uncle—her brother—used to "tease" her about it and sometimes talked disparagingly about Sicilians. It would take many more years for me to understand how those behaviors were rooted in anti-Blackness. Words like "terroni", which in Italian is an insult, yet it means of the land, would be used by Northern Italians to talk about Southern Italians. I remember realizing how I would only see Black Madonnas in Sicily and how washed out and pale Mary looked in Rome, where I was brought up during the school year. I had no language at the time to place those differences historically or culturally. I just knew that there were physical differences in my family, and especially between my parents' families, where my paternal grandmother was Slovenian, as well as differences in values and even the food we ate.

When I moved to England I was 22 and I had never lived by myself before. I remember the culture shock. People would ask, "how are you?" and keep walking without waiting for an answer. There would be queues for the bus, or for everything really, or so it felt, and I was alone. If I didn't understand something people would speak louder, sometimes slower, and get incredibly irritated. It was clear that I didn't belong here. All my friends initially were from other places: Greece, Turkey, Algeria, Bangladesh, India, and a few other Italians. Many of us stuck together, cooked for one another, and tried to make the immigrant experience a little less lonely.

It would be a few years still before I'd have a framework to understand how deeply political this experience was. In the meantime, I was told to gesticulate less, write more like an English person and not an Italian (my sentences were too long, they probably still are), and that I was untrustworthy in relationships because I was "hot-blooded" as an Italian and I would "naturally" cheat or break hearts. It was a time of confusion and not knowing who I was in many ways. I was also trying to make sense of my queerness and I hadn't yet come across bisexuality. In many ways my early 20s felt like floating at sea without a raft and without any land in sight. Unmoored, I was trying to make sense of living in several liminal spaces. I talk more about how this changed over time in the next section.

MJ writes...

Probably the first non-binary experience to impact me in a big way was being from a mixed class background. However this concept was not something people ever talked about back then, or even have much awareness of now. Also, because I was bullied for it, I held onto a lot of shame about class. For these reasons, it was actually a long time after coming out as bisexual—and later non-binary—that I started to recognize the resonances between my sexuality and gender and my class experience, and to consider them all together in terms of how they impacted my life.

Mixed class experience is probably pretty common, as many people's parents come from at least somewhat different backgrounds in terms of wealth, education, living situation, and the other things that we tend to associate with class. For me it was pretty profound as my dad's parents were working class and my mum's were upper class. Dad's dad was a carpenter and dad's mum had to go out to work, whereas mum's dad was a mill owner and mum's mum could focus on childcare. When I was a kid dad's parents lived in a small bungalow and mum's parents in a mansion house with a swimming pool! Everything was different in the two locations: the TV shows they watched, the food they ate, the conversations they had. For me it led to a strange sense of not-quite-fitting in either place, and not really understanding why. Both sets of grandparents struggled with our family for different reasons. Also there was a sense of difference for me with both my parents, given that my class experience was so different to theirs.

Being mixed class came together with other non-binary aspects of my experience in the ways I was bullied for my difference at school. People picked up that I was gender non-conforming, that my class set me apart, that I wasn't quite from the South or from the North because my accent was "wrong". Hearing difficulties that didn't quite pass the threshold for counting as a disability at that time compounded the isolation.

Reflection point: Existing in between, both/and, or beyond binaries

Having read our stories, think for a moment about any ways in which your identities or experiences could be seen as falling between binaries, or having elements of "both", or being beyond conventional binaries. If you like you could write your own paragraph about what these experiences were/are like for you.

It's important to recognize the differences between diverse non-binary identities and experiences on these various axes. Being mixed race comes with very different implications to being mixed class, or mixed ethnicities, for example. Being mixed race generally entails being much more visible, meaning that people often experience the discrimination due to being mixed, alongside the racism of being seen as a person of color in wider culture. Non-binary gender experiences differ from bisexuality, not least in being—at times— less culturally intelligible, and gender being potentially much more visible and policed on a daily basis through pronoun and bathroom use, for example.

However, it can also be useful to recognize some of the common features of these non-binary experiences, because this can help us to understand and make sense of what we've been through. Shared features of many non-binary experiences include:

- a sense of not completely fitting in either place (e.g. in straight or gay communities; with the sides of the family

who have different faiths; with white or Black family members)
- double discrimination from both sides of the binary (e.g. not being seen as middle class enough for middle-class communities, or working class enough for working-class communities)
- being regarded with suspicion with stereotypes such as being manipulative, indecisive, immature, greedy, and/or a betrayer (e.g. bisexuality being regarded as a phase; non-binary genders as being inauthentic)
- internalized shame due to a sense of there being something wrong about you (bisexual, non-binary, and mixed race people all suffer higher rates of mental health problems than those who fit dominant culture's binary categories of sexuality, gender, and/or race)
- trouble locating yourself in terms of privilege and oppression, given that your non-binary status likely results in complicated combinations of privilege and oppression experiences (e.g. bisexual people being read as straight when with a partner of the "opposite-gender" affording them some privileges and rendering a vital part of them invisible; light-skinned mixed race people being read as people of color, or white, depending on the context or country they're in)
- not knowing where you belong, or if all of you can belong anywhere (e.g. feeling like you can only bring a part of yourself to a place or community, or even to your family and friends).

Intersectionality

Intersectionality is a model that helps with unpacking some of this complexity. It was first introduced, in the late 1980s, by

Kimberlé Crenshaw, a Black legal scholar in the US, to describe the experiences of Black women in the criminal justice system, and how they differed from those of white women or Black men. The idea of intersectionality has a strong influence on us as authors. However, it's vital to acknowledge that it was born from Black feminism due to the marginalization of Black voices within a largely white, Anglo-American feminist movement. When applying it to other areas it is important never to forget its roots in racial justice and feminism.

Intersectionality can help us to think about where we're located in relation to cultural binary identity categories such as male/female, gay/straight, black/white, white collar/blue collar, disabled/non-disabled, trans/cis, rich/poor, urban/rural, old/young, and so on. Specifically it can help us to consider where our location in relation to these binaries places us in terms of power and privilege. Intersectionality is often misunderstood as being about how different aspects of our individual identities operate together to shape our experience, but actually it's about how interlocking systems of power impact us through patterns of privilege and oppression. Key intersectional thinkers Patricia Hill-Collins, Audre Lorde, and bell hooks all argue that binary either/or thinking is a key influence on oppression which intensifies dominance and marginalization.

Even for those whose identities or experiences are not explicitly non-binary, binary understandings of any aspect of our experience are challenged by intersectionality. This is because people experience any aspect of themselves very differently depending on their other identities and background, and how that is located in terms of wider social structures and power. For example, being a white, middle-class trans woman differs hugely from being a working-class trans woman of color, meaning that their priorities and lived experiences are likely to be very different. Consider how accessible medical treatments might be to them, or their everyday risk of violence, for example.

Thought experiment: Mapping your intersections
Take some time now to map your own key intersections in terms
of background, identity, and experience. You might want to draw
a mindmap, or simply list where you're located in relation to race,
class, gender, sexuality, faith, age, disability, geographical location,
generation, culture, ethnicity, and any other categories that feel
relevant. You might like to do one map for where you were at on
these things when you came into the world, and another for where
you're at now. We'll look more at the features that change over time
in the next section.

Given that we're particularly focused on non-binary experience
here, consider where your location in relation to these intersecting
aspects places you on a spectrum from privilege to oppression. Or
perhaps it's more complex than that and your location both privileges
you in some ways and oppresses you in others in terms of wider social
systems and structures. We'll come back to the privilege/oppression
binary in Chapter 6.

Borderlands

We have talked earlier about how both of us have experienced
existing in liminal spaces, of belonging and not belonging to
different categories, identities, and experiences. For many people,
such as people who live at the edge of settler colonial borders, the
liminal place can be very concrete. Gloria Evangelina Anzaldúa,
an American Chicana lesbian activist and scholar, who grew up at
the Texas/Mexico border, wrote clearly and cogently about these
experiences in *Borderlands/La Frontera: The New Mestiza*. Even
though her writing is very specific to "todos mexicanos on both
sides of the border" as she writes in her book's dedication, we would
be remiss if we did not mention this seminal work, given that there
is now a whole field of study dedicated to borderlands.

The experience of living in two places at once is very specific.
Anzaldúa also writes about existing between categories such as

men and women and straight and queer identities and experiences. Living at the borders, whether political, geographical, historical, linguistic, or social, changes us. Of course which borders we live across also make a difference. Living between political borders, such as the border between Mexico and the US, is a different experience than living between cultural and/or linguistic heritages. Yet, as we said earlier, there are also commonalities.

When we live at the borders, we often have to learn to navigate two cultures, two languages, two histories, two social norms, and more. As we do so, a third experience arises, the experience of navigating those realities. Living at the borders becomes its own distinct experience, which goes beyond the binary of belonging to one place or another.

Alex, for example, remembers their child watching *Inner Workings* directed by Leo Matsuda and produced by Sean Lurie. In this short film, there is a fight between heart and brain on which activity to take part in. Leo Matsuda talks about being Japanese-Brazilian in the extras on the DVD and how this informed *Inner Workings*. Alex's child talked about how she loved this and how she related to it. She felt it depicted some of her own experiences and feelings as someone who is half-Italian and half-English, as she describes herself. Over the past decade, she has also had the experience of being brought up in the US, having a Minnesotan accent, yet now trying to decide whether she even belongs there, as someone who has had a firm sense, since very young, that she was an immigrant.

More recently she spoke about how she enjoys talking to one of her friends who is Somalian. They're finding that their grandmothers are quite similar, as are their families, in many ways. They don't look like each other, as Alex's child is clearly white and the other child Black, and they don't come from the same culture, yet they also share some experiences around talking a different language than their grandparents, being bilingual, and having a family that works differently than the US Anglo families around them.

It feels vulnerable to even write this. We don't want you to think that we can all get along and get past the realities of racism, settler colonialism, and the violence of geopolitical borders. There are stark and undeniable differences. The impact of these borders is lethal on Indigenous, Black and Brown bodies, and we never want to forget this. And there are also experiences that happen when we live in the cracks, in these liminal spaces, in two places at once, that are unique and yet shared, defying the very same borders that dominant culture tries to carve into both the land and our bodies.

4.2 Fluidity and going beyond binaries over time

When we talked about gender and sexuality in the first two chapters of this book we discussed non-binary-ness in terms of being between/both/beyond binaries at one point in time, and also in terms of shifting between and beyond binaries over time. In this section we explore how the idea of fluidity—or change over time— applies to other aspects of experience like age, faith, migration, and changing social status. Thinking about our experiences across time we can see that many of them are non-binary in that they shift between and beyond binaries over the course of our lives.

Alex writes...

I wrote earlier of feeling how I didn't belong when I moved to the UK. After living there for 15 years, and experiencing xenophobia in several settings (work, relationships, friendships, queer community, health and legal systems), I moved to the US in 2008. One of the things that was clear as the brightest day when I moved was that I was now benefiting from white privilege in a way that was very different than the previous 15 years. In the US, I was clearly considered white by most people. My whiteness might be a little more conditional because of my accent, and therefore more easily revoked, but my day-to-day life was suddenly easier in many ways. This was a different kind of culture shock. When I tried to connect with Italian community in Minneapolis, I found it challenging to navigate it as a trans non-binary person, who, at the time, was still learning how to bring my whole being into different places.

In addition to this, because of a history of segregation in the US and assimilation into whiteness, I suddenly found myself navigating life surrounded by a lot of white people who had been brought up in an Anglo-dominant culture. Many of them clearly wanted me to be just like them, just a white person. I feel my experience is a little more complicated than that, as I was raised in a fairly community-based culture, for example, and not in a highly individualistic one like the US. It took time, and it feels vulnerable again, to admit that I had different experiences than most white US people who are my age. I had experienced xenophobia, I had been exocitized and othered, patronized and discriminated against, while living in the UK, because of my ethnicity, my accent, and my citizenship.

My experience as an Italian immigrant with white privilege in the US was therefore a little different than that of people who might have shared that experience at a different point in time. What this all means, I am still unpacking everyday. What I know is that my main focus right now is on how to be an immigrant on colonized land and what my responsibility is to the land, to the people Indigenous to that land, and to my child.

Another part of my identity that has shifted over time revolves around my health. In my early 20s I started getting inexplicably sick and fatigued. I also developed adult-onset asthma. Around that time, I was doing my PhD on disability and gender, and I identified as not disabled. After a few years of doctors' visits and tests, I was diagnosed with fibromyalgia, just before I turned 30. I now identify as having invisible disabilities and I still struggle to dismantle the unavoidable internalized ableism, while continuing to advocate for disability justice. Sometimes I struggle with whether "I'm disabled enough" to claim my identity as a disabled person. Other days, when even getting out of bed seems the most challenging of tasks, and might not even be achieved, I feel it's okay. I even questioned whether I have fibromyalgia at all when I have a good few weeks. Yet, the symptoms always return, the flare ups happen, no matter how careful I am, or how hard I try. I have also learned how my complex post-traumatic stress disorder (CPTSD) and developmental trauma impact me and how they change my capacity to show up in the world in many of the ways which are expected by dominant culture.

Internalized ableism still pushes me to seek for a "cure", to be well, to do more, to view my body as more worthy when it can produce something. Some days I am afraid my body will just give up and collapse. Those are the days when I know I need to slow down and make sure I'm not treating my body like an object: a commodity to use and be discarded. I am my body, there is no separation. Those are the days I read and re-read my favorite disability justice advocates and writers, such as Jenny Morris and Eli Clare, to remember that it's okay to be just who I am.

Finally, one more piece of my identity that has changed over time is about parenting. When I gave birth to my child I knew I was some sort of queer in terms of gender, and definitely in terms of sexuality. However, I had the misguided notion that to be genderqueer I had to be androgynous, which I clearly was not. This means that I was still identifying as cis and as somewhat gender conforming. When I gave birth to my child I was a mom. To her, I am still mom because she does not believe this should be a gendered role. I'm her mom and also a trans masculine person. She says my mom and "he" (I use both they and he pronouns) to refer to me in the same sentence, with the ease of someone who has been doing this for the past ten years.

I went from being a mom who had a challenging emergency c-section, breastfed, and brought my child into this world, to an invisible non-binary parent. How do you access resources when they're clearly marked as being for women, when you're not? Do I attend the workshop on dealing with the grief of having had a c-section and risk being potentially misgendered, or do I sit with that experience alone? How much energy do I spend telling my friends that just because she calls me mom, they still need to use my pronouns? I understand that is counter-cultural, but they too can uncouple the role of mother from a specific gender. Many of the other non-binary parents I know were already identifying as such when their children were born. I was a mom first, and now I'm still figuring out where I fit. The only person who seems not very challenged by this is my child. I'm her mom, and I'm trans, and she has lived in liminal spaces with me her whole life.

MJ writes...

For me gender, age, and mental health have shifted over time in ways that make them fluid rather than static, and plural rather than singular, experiences. They all also intersect with each other in ways that make them impossible to tease apart.

I could tell a linear narrative of all three of these things, which would fit better into larger cultural stories. For age that would be the obvious story of growing older over time: each year being one year older, more mature, and more experienced than the previous year. For gender that would be a trans narrative from being brought up as a girl and feeling that something about that didn't quite fit, to becoming more butch or masculine in my 30s, and eventually identifying as trans masculine and non-binary and going through some social and physical transitions (name and pronoun change, surgery, and taking some hormones). For mental health I could tell a recognized tale of recovery, from the events of my childhood that "caused" my mental health struggles, through experiences of depression and anxiety in my 20s and 30s, to many of these difficulties lifting in recent years as I worked on myself therapeutically and spiritually.

The danger of these kinds of linear cultural stories is that we can feel pressured to conform to them, for example to access services or to present ourselves as "successful" selves, even when they aren't a great fit. That can leave us feeling like imposters, or unable to access more complex narratives which might help us to understand and embrace our experiences better.

Let me share a different narrative through age/gender/mental health which has come to feel a much better fit for me. In this story I see myself as having multiple selves—rather than just one. However, some sides of myself were disowned or rejected at certain ages when I learnt they were not acceptable. For example, I left behind a vulnerable masculine self, when I was bullied at school because I learnt that a "girl" could not be that. I left behind a cocky confident masculine self a little while after, when the lack of acceptance I felt at school and home made me feel like I wasn't okay. Sometime in childhood I also left behind a very small, traumatized, side of myself which it just didn't feel safe to be. Disowning those parts of myself meant foregrounding other parts in order to survive what was happening to me: particular a strong inner critic and a people pleaser who would do anything to be accepted, including learning how to do "acceptable femininity". This was a huge part of my mental health struggles as the critical voices were overwhelming at times, tipping me into depression and self-harm.

During the last few years I've been exploring and reclaiming the sides of myself that got left behind through therapy, creative writing, and forms of meditation. This means that my self now feels like it has multiple sides which have different ages and genders. The vulnerable masculine side is a young teenager, the cocky masculine side an older one, and there is this small, queer person who holds a lot of trauma and also a lot of joy. I can embody those different sides meaning that I—and people around me—experience me as a variety of genders and ages. All of this is helping me to a better place in terms of my mental health and—at the same time—can leave me quite raw and vulnerable, experiencing feelings that got locked in the past. The whole thing is complex and fluid.

We'll come back to the idea that we—as selves—are plural and in process in Chapter 6. Meanwhile reflect on your experiences of fluidity in relation to your identity, body, and history.

Reflection point: Fluid experiences

Which aspects of your identity, body, and experiences have shifted over time? Which have remained static? Think about the wider cultural narratives about the way people are expected to change and develop over the lifecourse (e.g. maturing and settling down over time, becoming more successful over time, recovering from difficulties over time). Which of these stories fit your experience, and which feel like a less good fit? Which of these stories do you struggle with, and which do you accept with ease? Maybe it's the same stories, as we can have paradoxical feelings about any aspects of our experience.

Thinking about time

We've been talking about how some of our identities and experiences have changed over time, and invited you to reflect on how yours might have also changed. However, what is our notion of time? Can we say that there is a universal definition of time? It will come as no surprise whatsoever that we don't believe there is one.

The way we conceptualize time is deeply linked to cultural norms. For example, do we think of time as bipartite or tripartite? That is do we think that there is only past and present, given that the future is only potentiality, but does not exist until it does? Or do we think that there is a past, present and future, and that we're marching inexorably towards that future?

In addition to this, do we think of time as linear or circular, or as a spiral where we do not quite go back to the same place but maybe revisit patterns? And what about natural time, that is the time of the seasons, the stars, the sun and moon, as opposed to human time, which we arbitrarily measure by several units, calendars and clocks?

Where do our ideas of time come from? How have they been impacted by settler colonialism or not? If our idea of time is not the same as the idea of time in dominant culture, how does that impact us? We're aware that we have just thrown many questions out there, but hopefully you will find them useful, as you keep considering going beyond either/or being. In fact, we'd argue that we live both in natural time and human time. We look at clocks to make appointments and go about several parts of our day. Yet, we also notice what the weather is doing and dress accordingly to this, and not just the calendar. We have a time within our body too. Our heartbeats, our breathing, our aging all have their own pace. We exist within multiple types and constructs of time, without much effort.

Trans time

Another way of looking at time is trans time. Kat Gupta and Ruth Pearce have been exploring this concept in their work. First they point out that the way trans people are treated often denies them important experiences of time that other people can access. For example, the way that the media often continue to misgender trans people when reporting about them can be seen as refusing them the possibility of a future in their gender. At the same time, popular trans narratives may mean that they feel they have to erase their pasts. Policies and practices also expect trans people to be clairvoyant: promising to remain a certain way forever, if they are to access services or name-changes, for example. Finally, the lack of sufficient services for trans people means that those seeking physical transition often feel like their life is delayed—or on hold—while they wait for treatment.

However, trans people have found many ways to travel, trick, and transcend time. For example, trans people often experience non-linear life-courses which include disruption, disjuncture, and discontinuity of time. They might go through more than one puberty, with the second adolescence occurring later in life, and being experienced in a range of ways by different people. Many trans people also look younger than they are. Some talk of their age in terms of "trans years": the number of years since they came out. So trans people of the same chronological age who came out at different ages are likely to have vastly different trans time experiences, which belie their apparently similar age. MJ's example of reclaiming differently gendered sides of themselves, and having new beginnings at different points in time, is another example of trans time.

Of course such experiences of time are not necessarily restricted to trans people, or to cultures which have diverse understandings of time, it's just that other groups may be more stuck in dominant cultural narratives about linear time. It can be useful to think about how all of us might relate to our past and future selves, for example, or experience life as a series of mini-births and mini-deaths, or live in spirals or cycles rather than linear paths from A to B.

Slow down!

Talking about time, let's take some time to actually be with our bodies!

We invite you to take a few moments to make yourself comfortable. Notice your breathing, you don't need to change it, just notice it. Is there a way in which you could bring yourself to being even 1 percent more comfortable? If so, please take the time to do so.

Once you feel as comfortable and settled as you can be in this moment, and if you're able to do so, take some time to gently pat or squeeze your arms and hands, and even your legs and feet. If it feels more comfortable to just move your arms and legs, you can do that instead, or even just breathe and focus on different parts of your body.

As you do this, take a moment to offer gratitude to your embodied self for all the things you can do. We know there might also be things you cannot do, but what can you be grateful to your body for in this moment? Maybe it's just your breath, and that's enough. Maybe it's the hope you can feel gratitude again some day, and that's enough.

If you can, after doing this, think of a daily practice you could develop to show your body more love and gratitude. If you cannot think of one, that's okay. Maybe you can choose to breathe intentionally at the beginning of every day. Just being is enough.

When you're ready, feel free to keep on reading.

4.3 Disability and normal/abnormal, ill/healthy binaries

We mentioned both in the introduction and then through Alex's experience how our health status might change over time. For many people, of course, it's a both/and. People might be born with a disability, and then also have their health change over time. However, dominant culture is pretty keen to divide our bodies into disabled/abled, normal/abnormal, and ill/healthy, even though our bodies contain multitudes of experiences and complexities.

The boundaries of these binaries seem to be fragile and easily crossed, yet very challenging to navigate. People often struggle with knowing if they're "sick enough" to stay home from work or school, for example. Many people with chronic health issues seem to struggle with whether they do, or even *can,* consider themselves disabled. Many people struggling with severe mental health issues may or may not consider themselves disabled, even though they might really struggle with feeling "normal".

Those binaries are clearly arbitrary and incredibly dependent on so many contexts. For example they're dependent on the messages we were brought up with around health and sickness, as well as the difference between physical, sensory, and emotional capacity—and the legal requirements around these. They're also dependent on the various intersections we inhabit. For example disabled people of color and Indigenous people might have very different experiences to white disabled people. Feminine or masculine disabled people's experiences also seem to differ from one another, given the different societal gendered expectations of bodies. For example, studies have shown that if in an "opposite gender" married couple a woman develops a disability, the husband is more likely to leave compared to the reversed scenario.

Multiple experiences: Many ways of relating to disability

- "I never know if I can use the Disability suite at my favorite convention or not. I live with extreme anxiety. It has impacted every aspect of my life, from work to my relationships with my family and to my desire to go on living. But still I cannot bring myself to say I'm disabled. It feels like I'm cheating or something. I don't know if I'm being mindful of my privilege or if I just have a ton of internalized ableism honestly."

- "I find the disability and Deaf labels incredibly powerful. I was brought up to think there was something really wrong with me because of my Deafness, so when I found Deaf community, sign language and Deaf pride, it was revolutionary. I know many Deaf people don't consider themselves disabled. I agree that we're a linguistic and cultural group in our own right. However, I also want to draw attention to how I'm disabled by society, that's why I like using both disabled and Deaf."

- "It has been challenging to find healthcare providers that are competent in both autoimmune issues and working with Native people. Services that specialize in serving Native communities where I live don't seem very knowledgeable around my disability issues, and healthcare providers who understand my disability, don't understand my identity as an Ojibwe two spirit person."

- "I've become more and more withdrawn. I get scared that if I do something, I will be too exhausted to go to work the next day. That means all I'm doing is working and going to health appointments to manage my health. I'm exhausted, bored, and angry. My friends have stopped calling and I don't blame them. I don't want to be disabled but I think I am. Then I feel ashamed for not even wanting to be disabled, and that doesn't help."

- "I don't want to tell everyone I have a social communication disorder. So people think I'm always moody or have a temper. It's just hard to explain to people what's going on with me when actually communication with people is the main thing that's 'wrong' with me! I'm glad I know other people who struggle with this. It's so much more relaxing to be around them, they get it."

> ### Thought experiment: Health and disability
> *Think about your own experience of health and disability. Do you regard yourself as somebody with chronic health issues, or particularly prone to certain acute ones? Would you say that you had a disability or not? Draw a spectrum from ill to well, or disabled to not-disabled. Where would you place yourself now? Does this differ over time or does it remain relatively static? Is it different when you consider different parts of your body or emotional experience?*
>
> *We've focused mainly on physical health in this chapter, and mental health in the next one, however of course this is another binary that we need to challenge. The two are interconnected and inseparable, as we'll see. Trauma and emotional struggles are deeply embodied, and things that are conventionally understood as physical—like pain—take a huge emotional toll and are very influenced by our psychological responses to them.*

Thinking socially about disability

One way of looking at disability which profoundly challenges the binary model of people being either disabled or not disabled is the social approach. Social models of disability locate disability in society rather than in the individual. For example, stairs are something that *disable* people, rather than disability residing in the body of an individual person who uses a wheelchair.

Limits on people's capacities to conduct activities that are essential to everyday life are imposed by structural and systemic barriers. These barriers are part of a social system that regards some bodies as "normal" and some as "other", rather than considering a broad range of bodies and possibilities, for example when designing a building or piece of furniture. This relegates people with disabilities to the status of lesser citizens because of their lack of access.

Disability is a byproduct of a society which is organized around only certain bodies which are defined as "normal", in laws, education, institutions, and in popular culture. If we take this position then we might focus any solutions around societal interventions rather than medical ones designed to make a body conform more closely to particular norms. For example, providing people with audio or captions would be seen as enabling access to a wider community, rather than addressing a specific individual need.

Finally, social models of disability regard all of us as interdependent, rather than suggesting that people with disabilities are dependent in order to shore up a myth of everybody else being independent. Being reliant on a carer, for example, is part of a wider system of interdependency which includes the reliance that everybody has on those who produce our food, remove our garbage, and run public transport. The cultural emphasis on health and being "normal" place bodies with disabilities at the margins because people don't want to be reminded of their interdependency, limitations, pain, and mortality.

So following a more social model we might:

- be critical of binary thinking which differentiates between people without/with disabilities ("normal" vs. "other")

- shift our understanding of disability from a lack/impairment of specific bodies, to an understanding that a diverse range of bodies exists
- shift from locating disabilities within individuals to within society
- regard everyone as interdependent—rather than dividing dependent disabled people from independent non-disabled people.

Reflection point: Your body and the wider world

Think about your body in relation to the wider world around you, including any disabilities and your different sensory capacities, as well as your shape, size, and anything else that feels relevant. In what ways does the world enable you access? In what ways does it limit it? You might want to consider things like public transport, shops, buildings, and furniture, as well as cultural norms about the kinds of activities you "should" be able to engage with and how those impact you.

4.4 Bodies that matter and don't

We've mentioned in the previous section that disability is a byproduct of a dominant culture that defines certain bodies as "the norm". Health is not the only criteria that dominant culture uses to define what "normal" is. If we take psychological tests, for example, those are often "normed"—that is tested and validated—by carrying out research with college students in the US and Canada. These tend to be younger, wealthier, whiter, and generally not disabled. However, the psychological tests are then taken and used with a much broader range of people and even across national borders, when the same language is used.

In the past few years, we have seen several movements highlighting how certain bodies are viewed as "the norm", and therefore protected, and how other bodies are treated as disposable. One of the largest movements in the US and the UK has been the Black Lives Matter movement. This movement brought attention to the existing disparities—when it comes to loss of life as well as other issues—between Black and white people. The backlash of All Lives Matter shows absolute ignorance of these disparities. Whereas white parents do not need to fear for the lives of their white children when they're out playing, or driving a car, Black parents cannot avoid this worry and are often devastated by grief as yet another Black child is killed by the police. The Black Lives Matter movements never denied that all lives are sacred, but rather highlight that Black lives are not being treated as sacred, and that Black and Brown bodies are not only considered disposable in Hollywood movies but also in everyday life, and subject to systemic violence and murder by systems that were never meant to protect them in the first place.

There has already been a significant body of work developed by feminists of color, and especially Black feminists, on how "womanhood" in much of feminism usually means "white womanhood". For example, after the last presidential elections in the US in 2016 there were several "Women's Marches". Despite "good intentions", several trans women, Indigenous women and women of color reported negative incidents occurring at the marches. Of course some women had an amazing time and different experiences. It's rare that something is either completely positive or negative. What these experiences of micro and macro aggressions illustrate though is who feels entitled to be in a certain space, and when, as well as who views themselves as central to a movement.

139

Many white cisgender women view themselves as the center of the women's liberation movement and can find it challenging to acknowledge both the existence and the significant contributions of trans women, Indigenous women, Black and Brown women, disabled women, and non-binary femmes. This can lead into various forms of essentialism. If the definition of "womanhood" centers around having a vagina, then some trans women are automatically excluded. However, if it centers around experiences connected to having a vagina, such as menstruating, giving birth, and so on, does it mean that women who cannot menstruate, or who have chosen not to have children do not belong to the movement? If vaginas are central, whose vaginas become important? Can Black, Brown and Indigenous women who have been both hypersexualized and objectified be viewed as subjects? Can trans women, especially trans women of color, who are disproportionately impacted by misogynistic violence really be discounted because they may or may not have genitals congruent with dominant social expectations?

What we're asking in this section is whose bodies matter and whose bodies don't. Historically, in both the UK and the US white bodies, especially Anglo bodies, have mattered more, as have cisgender bodies, non-disabled bodies, masculine bodies, middle- and upper-middle-class bodies, thin bodies, younger bodies, and straight bodies. We know this from statistical evidence in relation to health disparities, discrimination, and violence. We also know this from people's accounts and the bodies that are predominantly represented in mainstream media.

Which bodies are portrayed as being the "norm" and which bodies are displayed in objectifying ways? For example, are Black, Brown, Indigenous, trans, disabled, and queer bodies only on display when murdered or in pain? Are they only displayed as a spectacle, rather than as part of the range of human experiences? Who are we paying attention to? For example, many white women felt very impacted by the TV series of the *Handmaid's Tale*, something they see as a dystopic future which might be coming dangerously close. However Black women in the US have already lived that future in their past, when during slavery their bodies were used non-consensually for reproductive purposes. Who is represented, in which context, and how? Whose story is being told and centered? Who controls the narrative? Who is telling the story, taking the picture, making the movie?

> ### *Thought experiment: Paying attention to the stories all around us*
>
> *For the next few days, take a few moments to notice the images and stories around you. Whose bodies are represented? Whose stories are being told and how? Feel free to use the questions in the paragraph just before this thought experiment. If you can, journal your observations. If there are bodies that are not represented in the media you already consume, is there a way in which you can seek out those images and/or stories? If you already do so, or start doing so, can you notice how this change in whose stories you listen to and which images you consume impacts you? We have some resources at the end of this chapter around visual diet, so feel free to check these out either before or after you carry out your own experiment.*

"Attractiveness"

Another binary which strongly influences how people are treated in dominant cultures is the attractive/unattractive, or beautiful/ugly binary. While people perhaps recognize that this is not a totally either/or binary, binary thinking still informs the sense that there is a spectrum where we could locate people in terms of their appearance. The idea of rating ourselves, or each other, on a scale of one to ten, or somebody being "out of our league" comes from this way of thinking. Apps where we swipe on potential partners solely based on appearance do little to help with this way of seeing things.

Among those who manage to match up to the "beautiful" body ideal, very few actually feel attractive and there's often a lot of anxiety about maintaining this beauty. If you are "beautiful" it's very tempting—in a culture which values beauty so highly—to define yourself in that way and to get all your validation from being that. Of course this means defining yourself by something which will inevitably change. Even if you avoid the kinds of accidents or illnesses that suddenly alter appearance, nobody can avoid the aging process, which takes us away from ideals that regard beauty as synonymous with youth.

For the much larger proportion of people, vast amounts of time and energy can be put into striving towards the beauty ideal, and much pain associated when it's unattainable. Just think about the extent of ridicule and rejection still attached to being "ugly" in our culture. However, it's hard to criticize this binary—and the pain it causes—because there's a strong cultural idea that being into looks is just fine because we are choosing it and because it's fun, pampering, or even empowering.

Ideals of attractiveness also often obscure racism, misogyny, ageism, and ableism. For example, on dating and sex apps many white gay men still think it's acceptable to say they are not interested in people from certain racial groups, or to fetishize people from particular groups, using the excuse that this is just what they're "naturally" into or not. Of course none of us can actually step outside of culture and escape the influence of narrow beauty ideals which present slim, young, white, non-disabled bodies as aspirational, encouraging everyone to judge themselves on the basis of how close the are to this ideal.

Appearance binaries give a clear sense of which bodies are seen as more valuable—as objects of desire, potential partners, or aesthetically pleasing—and which are not. As with disability, the world around us is also built around binary assumptions about normal bodies which do not fit the diversity of bodies which actually exist. For example, the discredited Body Mass Index (BMI)[1] is still used to judge the health of bodies, and many shops only stock clothing up to a size which is thinner than the average size, particularly for women.

Indigenous, Black, and Brown bodies are often non-consensually objectified, exoticized, and touched in public, especially, but not only, if presenting as feminine. It's as if bodies that "don't matter" in dominant culture become communal property of those that "do matter". Given that dominant culture is rooted in settler-colonialism and racism, this injustice and aggression make bone-chilling sense. We have not yet eradicated colonization and slavery of these bodies from our collective mind and culture, yet many of us refuse to understand how we keep those atrocities alive in our everyday lives.

Dwarf activists like Eugene Grant point out how public transport, buildings, stores, and so on rarely consider the height range of people who will be accessing them, and how the vast majority of the general public still deem it acceptable to comment on a dwarf person's appearance, to take photographs of them, or to ridicule them as though they were not even a fellow human being.

Fat activists point out very similar things in relation to the treatment of fat bodies in public, with the additional point that fat people are often blamed for their fatness despite much of the moral panic around "obesity" being based on myths and faulty

---

[1] For example BMI doesn't distinguish between muscle mass and fat mass, doesn't take account of a person's build, and doesn't work well across different heights. It has also been criticized for not being a good predictor of health outcomes.

evidence.[2] Stacy Bias's animation *Flying While Fat* reveals how deeply fat stigma is ingrained in society. It points out that plane seats have shrunk over the years to a size which is painful for many fat bodies. This pain is exacerbated by the negative responses of other passengers, which make fat people want to shrink themselves as much as possible and avoid moving around the plane—even if that causes them severe discomfort and jeopardizes their health.

This is a useful analogy for many other hierarchical binaries which value certain bodies more highly than others. If people whose bodies took up less space on planes could make more room for those who take up more space then everyone could be more comfortable, just as in other aspects life could be better for everyone if people who were more privileged and powerful could share some of their power, instead of hoarding it for themselves.

Reflection point: Your body

In which ways is your body regarded as more normal or ideal, more highly valued, or granted easier access, in wider culture? In which ways not? How does that impact on your experience of navigating the world? How might this change over time for you?

In the next chapter of the book, where we talk about emotions, we say more about the cultural mind/body split which is a big part of the reason that we tend to treat our bodies as surfaces to perfect in terms of appearance, or machines to be productive, rather than considering ourselves as embodied beings.

---

2   See Cooper, C. (2016) *Fat Activism*. Bristol: HammerOn Press.

Further Resources

You can read more about bodies from similar perspectives to the ones we explore here in the following books:

- Anzaldua, G. (2012) *Borderlands/La Frontera: The New Mestiza*. San Francisco, CA: Aunt Lute Books.
- Berhard, T. (2010) *How to Be Sick: A Buddhist-Inspired Guide for the Chronically Ill and Their Caregivers*. Somerville, MA: Wisdom.
- Clare, E. (2015) *Exile and Pride: Disability, Queerness, and Liberation*. Durham, NC: Duke University Press.
- Clare, E. (2017) *Brilliant Imperfection: Grappling with Cure*. Durham, NC: Duke University Press.
- Crenshaw, K. (2019) *On Intersectionality: Essential Writings*. New York: The New Press.
- Eddo-Lodge, R. (2017) *Why I'm No Longer Talking to White People About Race*. London: Bloomsbury Publishing.
- Hill-Collins, P. and Bilge, S. (2016) *Intersectionality*. Bristol: Polity Press.
- hooks, b. (2015) *Ain't I a Woman: Black Women and Feminism*. New York/London: Routledge.
- Lorde, A. (2013) *Sister Outsider: Essays and Speeches*. New York: Ten Speed Press.
- Morris, J. (1991) *Pride against Prejudice: Transforming Attitudes to Disability*. London: The Women's Press.
- Renee Taylor, S. (2018) *The Body Is Not an Apology: The Power of Radical Self-Love*. Oakland, CA: Berrett-Koehler Publishers.
- Serano, J. (2013) *Excluded: Making Feminist and Queer Movements More Inclusive*. Berkeley, CA: Seal Press.

- Shukla, S. (ed.) (2017) *The Good Immigrant*. London: Unbound Digital.

To apply these ideas more to your life, check out these resources:

- everydayfeminism.com
- thebodyisnotanapology.com
- Erica Hanna's Ignite talk on visual diet: https://youtu.be/Dfq4iU3x1ZM, accessed on 21 November 2018.
- Gender Stories' podcast. Alex Iantaffi interviews Erica Hanna about body image issues and sexual violence, amongst other issues: http://genderstories.buzzsprout.com/156032/717775-navigating-the-world-as-a-woman, accessed on 21 November 2018.
- Lillian Bustle's TED talk on Stripping Away Negative Body Image: https://youtu.be/ME-col8oTkY, accessed on 21 November 2018.

You can find out more about the work of some of the people mentioned in this chapter on their websites and on twitter:

- stacybias.net
- Ruthpearce.net
- Mixosaurus.co.uk
- twitter.com/mreugenegrant

CHAPTER 5

Emotions

In dominant culture, we often think of emotions as separate from our bodies and as something that we can control. In fact it almost seems desirable to control emotions since we can sometimes feel that, if we don't, they would maybe spill out all over the place! A part of our bodies that we have not quite talked about yet is our nervous system. Our emotions are deeply embedded in our bodies and nervous system, which is of course also part of our body.

If all of this sounds a little confusing, please don't worry; in this chapter we're about to go a little deeper as we address emotions as embodied experiences, how dominant culture has come to value rationality over emotional states, and why we think this is a damaging and dangerous binary. We'll also discuss moving beyond binaries such as positive vs. negative feelings, and finally dismantling the mad/sane binary so that we can move towards individual and collective emotional wellness.

5.1 The mind/body binary and embodied emotions

We made some potentially confusing and somewhat circular arguments in the introduction about bodies, emotions, and nervous systems, so let's unpack them in this section. As we've already discussed in the previous chapter on bodies, the separation between body and mind is not universal. This separation, in Western European and Anglo-dominant countries, can be clearly traced back to Descartes' philosophy in the 1600s. His theory is a form of rationalism, which centers thought as a way of knowing the world, rather than deriving our knowledge from direct sensory experiences.

Descartes' ideas led to the creation of the mind/body binary that is now so prevalent—and troublesome—in dominant culture. First of all let's clear something up: this not how our body works! The brain is a part of our body and only one part of our nervous system. The brain, together with our spinal cord, is part of our central nervous system, whereas the peripheral nervous system includes the autonomic and somatic nervous systems. The peripheral nervous system has nerves that go to arms, hands, legs, and feet from the spinal cord, as well as nerves that go to heart, lungs, stomach, intestines, bladder, and genitals. In the central nervous system there are nerves that go into the eyes, mouth, ears, and many other parts of our head. That is a lot of nerves and cells continuously carrying messages to each other.

What does this all have to do with emotions? Contrary to what Descartes thought, we do not exist as an organism with two separate systems—the mind and the body. Our mind is an integral part of our body. We are embodied beings, with embodied thoughts, emotions, and reactions. For example, when we're having anxious thoughts, we might notice our heart rate and breathing changing, we might experience sensations in our stomach, such as "butterflies" or tightening. In some situations we might also sweat, tremble, or have a sudden bowel evacuation (there is a reason why there is an expression about shitting our pants when we're afraid!) This is our nervous system at work.

We know we're having an emotion because we are having a physical, embodied experience. We might also have some thoughts that go along with the emotions but if we pay attention to our bodies, that is where the information is coming from. When we feel sad, for example, we might cry or experience heaviness in our limbs, making it hard to move and take action. When we're feeling anger, we might feel heat rising, trembling, and shaking, and we might also cry. Our emotions have somatic—that is bodily—expressions, which we may be more or less familiar with.

Our emotions are also influenced by the environment we're in and the way we move. It is a mutual and circular relationship in our body. We pick up signals from the environment and our body and carry messages to the brain about what's happening and vice versa. This is indeed a complex system and sometimes tracking what is happening with our emotions can become a little bit of a chicken and egg situation. For example, if we don't sleep very much or well, don't eat enough, drink adequate amounts of water, and move within our capacity, our mood is impacted. These emotions in turn impact our ability to sleep, eat, drink, and exercise. It is a dance we're in from our first to our last breath, and yet, for many of us, it's an unfamiliar dance in which we might feel out of control and scared.

Reflection point: How do you know what you feel?
Take a moment to slow down and notice what you're feeling. Maybe you're not feeling anything. That too is an emotion; it might be that you're feeling numb or content or other emotions that are a little challenging to track.

149

Wherever you're at, can you pay attention to your body? What is your heart doing? How is your breathing? What is happening in your stomach? How about your muscles? Are they tensed or relaxed? If you don't know the difference, you can try to squeeze your whole body as you breathe in and then relax and let go of the squeeze when you breathe out. If you do this a few times, you may be able to feel into the difference between your muscles being tight and tense and being relaxed as you let go.

Over the next few days you may want to pause and notice your emotions two to three times per day. What are you feeling? How do you know that you're feeling it? For example, if you feel excited, what are the sensations that let you know that you're excited? You can write down your experiences and get to better know your emotions and how they manifest somatically, that is in your body.

The impact of trauma on our emotional wellbeing

We've mentioned how for many of us the dance of emotions within our bodies can feel unfamiliar. It can also feel uncomfortable, unpleasant, to be avoided, or downright dangerous. This may be because our nervous systems have not had a chance to develop a sense of containment and ease. Alex, for example, was incredibly relieved to find out about CPTSD and developmental trauma, that is trauma that happens while our brains are still forming in childhood, adolescence, and even very early adulthood (before the age of 25 usually). Those labels finally explained many of their experiences, which were hard to make sense of previously. They also fitted with many of the experiences their clients were reporting in therapy.

One of the dangers of the false mind/body binary is that we can perceive the body as being under the control of the mind. However, this is then incongruent with the experience many of us have of being "out of control" when feeling strong emotions. When we experience strong emotions, in fact, we might get into a fight, freeze, or flight reaction. This means that we might experience feeling combative, argumentative, and aggressive and generally wanting to pick a fight with someone, or even hit an object, someone, or ourselves. In other situations, we might feel frozen and unable to act, to move, to get away. Or we might feel that getting away as fast as we can, whether physically or emotionally, is the best and only thing we can do. We might feel as if our life depends on it and that we have no other options. These are trauma responses.

We need our trauma responses in order to survive. If we're about to get attacked by a lion, we don't really want to sit and debate what the best course of action is, we just want to—and do—react "without thinking". What is actually happening is that other parts of our nervous system are doing the thinking, rather than just our prefrontal cortex, which is responsible for executive functioning such as planning and making decisions. The way we function, and our access to fight, flight, or freeze, is great to react to an attacking lion, but not so great when everything looks like a lion.

When some form of trauma happens early (developmental trauma) or severely and repeatedly (CPTSD), the problem is that everything might end up looking like a lion, including our loved ones as well as more neutral people and situations. There can be a lack of a felt sense of safety and containment, especially when we're out of our window of tolerance, that is, beyond our capacity to be with something.

Trauma is a big word and many people think that this needs to be something "severe", such as sexual and/or physical abuse. However, especially for children and adolescents, trauma can be emotional, such as being brought up by an emotionally absent parent or a parent who also had CPTSD or developmental trauma and did not have the tools to address this. The latter is quite common given that CPTSD and developmental trauma are relatively new concepts in neurobiology, psychology, and therapy.

Trauma can also be historical, cultural, and social. Many of us come into the world in a "cloud of trauma". For example, all of us in Western dominant culture come into a world that has split mind/body. We also come into a world where the male/female binary, as discussed in Chapter 2, causes its own cultural and social trauma. We come into a world where settler colonialism and racism have created other binaries, such as Black/white, which dehumanize Black and Brown bodies, as we discussed in Chapter 4.

This might mean that our emotions are not always helpful, tolerable, or even understandable. We might find it hard to sit with our emotions, or we might actively try to get away from them by distracting ourselves, numbing ourselves, or keeping busy all the time. We might watch too much TV, use alcohol or drugs to manage our feelings, or have a very busy schedule and yet feel we are both too much and never enough. When this happens, we might feel scared of our own selves and emotions, instead of being helpful guides, become demons to be avoided at all costs.

When emotions stop being helpful guides, we might get into other unhelpful binaries, such as categorizing emotions as good/bad and trying to avoid the bad ones, or categorizing ourselves as normal/crazy or worthy/unworthy, which can leave many of us feeling crazy or unworthy unless we prove ourselves again and again, and yet it is never enough. We might also find ourselves locked into all/nothing binary thinking. This means that we might find ourselves incredibly active and then collapsing when we cannot sustain that level of activity. We might think we're the best at times and the worst at other times. We might find it hard to start things but then, once we start, we might find it hard to stop and take breaks. We might need to keep going until we feel we have finished something, or we're simply too exhausted to carry on.

Needless to say, this can be scary. That is why Alex was so relieved to find out about CPTSD and developmental trauma. Here were ideas that made sense of disparate experiences and emotions! Another thing, which can be quite scary, is that we might feel like we "should" be able to do better if we were only "strong enough". Why can't we just override these emotions and reactions? Why do some of us feel we're inside of a train wreck and we're driving it but we can't stop it? That's because trauma reactions were never meant to be overridden by our prefrontal cortex, as one of Alex's *Somatic Experiencing*® instructors, Kathy Kain says.

If we see a lion, as we said earlier, we don't want to sit around making a plan, we need to react. Fight, flight, or freeze are part of our survival and are necessary. The point is not to never feel those reactions again but to not live in a state of constant stress, where we're surrounded by metaphorical lions all the time! Living in a constant state of stress is really impactful on us and our wellbeing, as the ACE (adverse childhood events) study has clearly shown. For example, we might get sick more often, our autoimmune system might not work properly, or we might be in a lot of pain because our bodies are bracing much of the time. However, because of the mind/body binary in dominant culture, we might get locked into the idea that we "should" do better and be more "rational", that it's our fault that we cannot feel better or do better. We address the emotional/rational binary in the next section of this chapter. In the meantime, after all this talk of trauma, we want to end this section with some hopeful news. In the same ways that trauma can be passed on generation to generation, and lives within our nervous system, healing wisdom can also be passed on and it's already within us. Our bodies—that is, we—are incredibly smart.

We have neuroplasticity, for example, which is basically the ability to retrain our nervous system and create new neural pathways. We're not destined to live in a state of constant stress, even if we have CPTSD or developmental trauma. Interestingly much healing from CPTSD and developmental trauma includes training ourselves to move away from binaries, given that trauma physiology wants to live at the extremes (good/bad; normal/crazy; do/don't; all/nothing). There is so much more to say about this and we've included some resources at the end of this chapter. This is but an introduction to the idea of emotions as somatic events, and why it's important to pay attention to the unhelpful binaries we might get stuck with emotionally.

Thought experiment: We were meant to go up and down

Over the next few days, take time to notice when your heart rate goes up or down, when your breathing is shallow and fast or slow and relaxed. This might be challenging, especially if you're used to thinking too much about your body because you're scared there might be something wrong with it. If that is the case, instead of observing yourself, start by observing a pet or other people, especially children.

What's happening in the body when you or someone else gets excited? Can you feel heat rising, your heart rate going up? Can you notice someone else's cheeks get red or that they're breathing faster? What's happening in your body when you or someone else is relaxed? Do you feel slower and calmer? Can you notice someone else's features when they are relaxed? Is their jaw less tense, their shoulders lower? Is their skin not as flushed. Is their breathing slower?

Take time to notice how nervous systems get aroused—that is, go up—and how they relax and let go—that is, come down. This is our organic rhythm: expansion and contraction. Our heart and lungs work this way too. They expand and contract, all the time, with each heartbeat and each breath. We get excited and eventually we need to come down. We're down and eventually we need to go towards movement to survive. If intense emotions feel scary, you may want to set a timer when you feel them and notice that the level of high intensity usually lasts no longer than a few minutes and then you start to come down a little. Of course we can always work ourselves back up! However, we can only sustain sobbing or hyperventilating, for example, for a certain period of time, then our nervous system has to come down and it will, if given time and, if needed, extra support by someone who can stay with us and remain calm, grounded, and present.

The goal of this activity is to start noticing that maybe you can trust your body, and your emotions, and therefore yourself, a little more each time you notice how you expand and contract, and how everyone else and everything else in nature does too.

5.2 Emotional vs. rational

We've mentioned that we live in Western dominant cultures that seem to place rationality as superior to emotional states. MJ lives in the UK and Alex currently lives in the US, after living in the UK for 15 years, and having been brought up in Italy for the first 22 years of their life. This means that we've both experienced different cultural, social, and historical contexts when it comes to emotions.

In our ever-evolving friendship we have at times come across the tension that can arise from having been brought up in very different paradigms. This tension is real and sometimes even painful, yet it cannot be easily solved by choosing which paradigm is "better". In fact if we went down that road, our friendship might not have lasted. It might come as no surprise at all, by this point in the book, to read that we don't think the emotional/rational binary is a helpful one. Too often the emotional/rational binary becomes a coded way to not only distance from emotions but also to perpetuate racism, classism, and misogyny. Let us break down why.

Who can safely display emotions?

Expressing emotions and the vulnerability that can come with doing so is not an even playing field. In *Daring Greatly*,[1] US author Brené Brown makes some compelling arguments for the power of vulnerability. While we agree with her in many ways, we've also found that we're not all equally vulnerable when we express emotions and make ourselves known. When Alex, for example, asked Brené a question about trans youth, and especially trans youth of color, and "enforced" vulnerability at an event, she agreed that there is a difference between those of us who "dare greatly" by entering an arena of our peers and those of us who face an arena of people who think they are the norm.

We used the term "enforced" vulnerability to indicate the fact that many marginalized people do not have the option to keep certain matters private, including our emotional states at times, given that many of us are scrutinized, objectified, and policed in ways—and with an intensity—that people at the heart of dominant culture are not. Basically, many of us are already vulnerable whether we like it or not. For survival, some marginalized folks might go with this and be completely open around their process, while others, also for survival, might not. As you can guess, in our opinion no one way is better than another.

Whichever survival strategy we choose, we're still living in a word where rationality is seen as superior to emotionality, especially in certain bodies. Whereas cisgender white Anglo straight people might be seen as "brave and vulnerable" when displaying their emotional states, many marginalized people, such as Black and Brown people, ethnic minorities, trans people, and disabled people, to name a few, might be seen as "angry and hostile".

At this point some of you might argue that it is "how" these

---

1   Brown, B. (2013) *Daring Greatly: How the Courage to Be Vulnerable Transforms the Way We Live, Love, Parent and Lead*. London: Penguin.

emotions are displayed that matter and that some of us are just "doing it wrong" and are indeed being "too angry". We talk more about tone policing in the next section. In the meantime, we'd like to propose that this is not the case and it's not the "how" but the "who" that matters. Who is safe to display some emotions and not others? Who benefits from a rhetoric of "rational discourse at all costs", even in the face of violent systemic oppression?

If we look at tropes and stereotypes, it becomes clear who is allowed what emotions. There is no stereotype of the "angry white woman" but there is one for both the "angry Black woman" and "the angry trans person" (especially trans women). For some people, such as Black trans women of color, displaying appropriate emotional reactions can be lethal.

For example, when CeCe McDonald, a young African-American woman in Minneapolis (US) defended herself in 2011, when attacked outside a bar by a white supremacist man with a history of violence, her act was not seen as self-defense but rather as murder. She accepted a plea of second-degree manslaughter in 2012 because the jury she would have faced was not a jury of her peers. The jury was not likely to see a young woman, a college student in her early 20s, in fear for her life after having had glass smashed on her face, but rather an angry and "dangerous" Black "man". Take a moment to imagine what would have happened if CeCe had been white and her attacker Black. There would likely have been no case and prosecution, given that this is what had happened in those kinds of scenarios in the past with the same prosecutor.

The case was hardly covered in the media but activists from many countries drew attention to it, including Leslie Feinberg and Laverne Cox. CeCe's story illustrates just how dangerous it can be for Black trans women to do what anyone else in that situation might do: draw on whatever is at hand to defend themselves, in this case a pair of sartorial scissors she happened to have in her bag, given that she was a fashion student in Community College at the time.

This case might seem extreme but its roots reside in anti-Blackness, transphobia, queerphobia, and misogyny. CeCe was expected to act rationally in a highly charged emotional situation. There was no expectation of the drunk cisgender straight white man who ran after her to have behaved more rationally. He was behaving as we often expect men to behave in dominant culture: violently and aggressively, displaying a degree of toxic masculinity we have not only been taught to tolerate but almost celebrate as an intrinsic trait of masculinity itself.

Race, class, and the rational/emotional binary

The binary of rational/emotional is at heart a racist and xenophobic one. Much of Anglo whiteness's sense of superiority to "others" comes from the ability to maintain a cool head in heated situations. Think about the line in the famous poem by Rudyard Kipling: "If you can keep your head when all about you are losing theirs"; not only is this linked to gender—"you"ll be a man, my son"—it is also linked to colonialism as Kipling also believed that the colonized should recognize their inferiority and accept their governed position, referring in another poem to the "white man's burden" governing "your new-caught sullen peoples, half devil and half child". This is, of course, clearly and explicitly racist. As such, we might think it's an exception. However, too often people equate rationality with moral rightness. For example, we might think that if we—or those around us—get too emotional, shout, or display a degree of emotionality that we find inappropriate, they're automatically "wrong", no matter what the situation is.

Alex, for example, took many years to realize how emotionally impacted they had been from moving to the UK from Italy at 22 years old. Suddenly they went from being a fairly quiet, introverted, bookish person to being seen as loud and aggressive for being direct and displaying emotions. This was, of course, not just about ethnicity, but also about class. It seems clear from many British TV shows, such as *Eastenders* and *Coronation Street* for example, that it is acceptable for working-class people to be loud, but not middle- and upper-middle-class people. However, class alone is not a sufficient explanation as, once again, there is a difference between white working-class people and Black and ethnic minority working-class people too.

Part of being assimilated into whiteness is to make our bodies stiffer and quieter, to suppress our emotions, because they are seen as inferior and "primitive" compared to the superior and "more evolved" state of rationality. Rational/emotional is therefore not just a binary but a hierarchical binary. Colonized bodies are bodies that are supposed to be under control, as we discussed in the previous chapter. Black and Brown bodies, as well as trans and disabled bodies in many ways, and especially those bodies at the intersection of these identities, histories, and experiences, are seen as "dangerous" and "defiant" of this hierarchical order, especially when displaying emotions.

Many Black activists, artists, and journalists in the US have, for example, discussed, and shown in shows like *Black-ish* and *Dear White People*, the way Black parents need to give the talk about racial bias to their children to keep them safe. Because Black children are not seen as children in US dominant culture, it is dangerous for them to be too emotional, or to behave similarly to white children, as this might have lethal consequences, such as being killed by the police, being incarcerated, or being removed from their parents' care. There is an "enforced" rationality that Black children need to learn at an early age to survive a system biased by the rational/emotional binary, in which their emotions—including playful and/or developmentally appropriate ones—are seen as potential threats. For example, 12-year-old Tamir Rice was shot and killed by police when playing with a toy gun, and Dymond Milburn—the same age—was beaten by police when she began screaming as they mistakenly tried to arrest her outside her house.

It is impossible therefore to talk about the rational/emotional binary without talking about power and privilege. Only some bodies can access the full range of the rational/emotional continuum without being denigrated, patronized, judged as inferior, or even assaulted or murdered. Sadly even if marginalized people were to behave "perfectly rationally", this would not be enough, as we have seen in case after case in the US of Black people and disabled people, especially those with severe mental health issues, being killed, often regardless of their actions.

At this point, you might feel a little overwhelmed. Don't worry, there is a "slow down page" between this section and the next one! It is indeed a lot to take on if you haven't thought about any of this before. This type of bias can be like the air we breathe. We unknowingly take it in and cannot help doing so. If you're impacted by those issues, you know them all too well and might feel triggered or exhausted by this section. Before we take a break though, we would like to offer a few words on this topic from a range of perspectives.

Multiple experiences: Which emotions are okay and where?

- "Growing up I felt like I had to behave differently if I visited some of my friends. Our house was loud and full of people most of the time, we could run around and play, unless we were told to be quiet for some reason. We all talked in Italian and English, sometimes even Spanish, depending who was visiting. Some of my friends' houses were so quiet and I always felt careful, like I was going to break something, just for being there."
- "Because I struggle with CPTSD, sometimes my startle

response is really strong. I might jump, make a sound, or even burst out crying if I am surprised by loud noises or sudden movements. People get so uncomfortable when I do that. Sometimes I cannot deal with the way people look at me when that happens, so I just avoid crowded places or people I don't know well. It's just not worth it. They make me feel like I'm crazy."

- "These white women at work are always talking about my colorful clothes and trying to touch my hair, sometimes openly, sometimes not. I'm so angry but I feel I cannot show it. I don't want to be seen as another 'angry Black woman' and, even more so, I'm scared of what would happen to my career, since I'm in a small field. I come home exhausted because I have to keep overriding my emotions and make it look like I'm okay when I'm not."

- "As a trans woman I always feel like I'm trying to make myself smaller and quieter. If I get excited, or take up 'too much space' because a topic is important to me, I often get accused of having been brought up with 'male privilege'. I see cis women do the same thing and they're seen as powerful and assertive by other women sometimes, but that's not the way they see me. Sometimes it feels like there can be no girl power or sisterhood for me."

- "I'm quite a 'soft man'. I've never liked rough and tumble play, I'm not loud or aggressive, and I have no desire to get into pissing contests with other men. Sometimes when I start crying it's like the floodgates have opened. I try to just let the tears come but it does freak people out. They think there's something really wrong with me. If I weren't so tall, people would probably see me as weak because I'm emotional. People thought I was gay growing up, because apparently if you're not that macho, you must be gay. It didn't bother me but it wasn't me."

Slow down!

Whatever your own identities, histories, and experiences, this might feel like the right time for a breather. It was a lot of emotions we've asked you to sit with already!

Take some time to slow down and breathe. As you breathe see if you can make your exhale, that is breathing out, longer than your inhale, that is breathing in. For example, if you're breathing in for the count of 1, 2, 3, you might want to breathe out for 1, 2, 3, 4, 5, 6.

Repeat this breathing pattern a few times. As you do this, notice what happens to your heart rate, your muscles, your thoughts and feelings. You may want to try this a few times to really notice how it impacts you.

The goal is to feel a little more relaxed and present. If you find yourself becoming more agitated or anxious, please stop and do something that you know works for you when you're upset. Then have a cup of tea, or hot chocolate, or some water, go back to your usual breathing pattern and carry on reading...

5.3 Beyond "positive" vs. "negative" feelings

Along with distancing from emotional experience entirely, one thing we commonly do is to separate emotional states into "positive" and "negative" versions and then endeavour to only feel the positive ones and none of the negative ones. We grasp hold of feelings like joy, excitement, contentment, and fulfilment, and hurl away ones like fear, anger, sadness, and shame.

This binary is particularly strongly felt by MJ because it has shaped their life in such powerful ways. MJ writes:

> My parents made a pact when they got together to only allow positive feelings and no negative ones. They both grew up with a parent who had significant mental health issues, meaning they were probably in the presence of some very volatile emotional expressions as children, which felt frightening and uncontrollable to be around. They figured that the way to deal with this was to train themselves—and their kids—out of difficult feelings.

> As a child I cried a lot, especially after we moved house around the age of five. Apparently my Mum asked my teacher what she should do about this, and the teacher recommended a "cry chart". Basically if I got through the day without crying I would get a star on the chart, and if I got enough stars in a week then I would get a comic or sweets at the end of that week.

> Far from training me out of crying—and the underlying emotions behind the tears—this strategy meant that I learnt that crying and sadness were unacceptable. If I ever expressed those feelings I knew that I had ruined the entire day, or even the week: there was no chance of getting that star back now. I learnt to feel shame and anger at myself for feeling tough feelings, which meant they spiralled and became a lot more painful and hard to handle.

Messages we receive about feelings

Before getting into the different emotional states in more detail, let's think about the messages we receive about feelings, which have a major impact on which emotions feel okay to experience or express, and which don't. You can see from MJ's example how cultural messages around appropriate levels of emotional expression came together with their parents' specific experiences of intergenerational trauma to result in a set of messages about the unacceptability and shamefulness of certain emotional states or expressions.

Figure 5.1: Multiple levels of gendered experiences

We find this diagram (Figure 5.1) super-helpful for reflecting on the messages we receive about all kinds of things. You could use it to think through your relationship to sex, gender, relationships, or your body, for example. Here let's use it to consider emotions.

CULTURE

On the outer level our wider culture gives us strong messages about which emotions it's okay to express or feel, and which it isn't. Generally, in Western dominant cultures, we're encouraged to express "positive" feelings and not "negative" ones. For example, the

British "stiff upper lip" discourages expressions of fear and sadness. North American culture often encourages stories of success and positivity, but not of struggles without a positive outcome. Also, messages differ depending on our individual identities, with certain emotions being seen as more or less acceptable for people of certain genders, classes, ages, or nationalities.

COMMUNITIES AND INSTITUTIONS

On the next level in, our communities and institutions also reinforce many of these messages. For example, in school we might have been judged for being too enthusiastic and uncool. In the workplace there might be no place for "becoming emotional" or we might be encouraged to look like we're all in a constant state of anxiety and overwhelm. We might have community norms about whether it's good or bad to express anger or jealousy.

It's easy to find ourselves joining in a kind of *tone policing* in our communities whereby certain emotions are deemed unacceptable to admit to or express—for certain people or across the board. It's worth being mindful of this whenever we find ourselves judging how somebody "should" or "shouldn't" feel about something.

INTERPERSONAL RELATIONSHIPS

At the interpersonal level we learn a great deal about acceptable and unacceptable feelings from our close relationships, particularly from the family and friends around us growing up.

It's important to remember that our parents—and the other close people in our lives—also live in the same wider culture as we do with all of its crappy messages about unacceptable feelings. They're also part of institutions and communities that have done a number on them. And they're in their own family systems wherein certain emotions have been deemed too dangerous or threatening. So they may well have responded by giving us a clear message that our fear, sadness, anger, joy, disgust, or other feelings, were not something that they could be around, that they couldn't love us if we expressed them, or that we should protect them from those feelings. Of course, as we said in the previous section, it is literally not safe for many marginalized people to express emotions, as this might put them in lethal danger from systems such as mental health institutions and the police.

Systemic therapy also talks about how people in family and friendship groups often become fixed in relation to certain feelings, for example as "the happy one", "the problem one", the person who has to worry about everybody, or the person who everyone is scared of upsetting. The system as a whole can keep us stuck there.

SELF

We will have internalized all of these messages from the other levels. Either we'll have managed to find a way of shutting down the "bad" emotions entirely, or—perhaps—in trying to shut them down we'll have managed to make them shout more loudly so we've become defined by them.

Reflection point: Your relationship to emotions
Try noting on the diagram (Figure 5.1) the messages you've received in the past—and receive now—about which feelings are "good" or "bad": which emotional experiences and expressions are acceptable and unacceptable.

Why are all feelings important?
The Pixar movie, *Inside Out,* is a great one for illustrating why the strategy of distancing from "negative" feelings and trying to only feel "positive" ones is damaging. The film follows an 11-year-old, Riley, and her emotions—Joy, Sadness, Disgust, Anger, and Fear—as her family moves from Minnesota to San Francisco. Previously

her inner world has been dominated by Joy. Joy has made it her business to ensure that Riley remains as happy as possible, building up a store of mostly joyful memories which have, in turn, shaped her personality. However, following the house-move, many of these memories become tainted by Sadness—who can't seem to stop themself from touching them and turning them blue.

In her attempts to prevent Sadness from causing any more damage, Joy manages to get both of them ejected from the control room to the outer reaches of Riley's inner world. This leaves Anger, Fear, and Disgust in charge while Joy and Sadness try everything they can to get back before Riley runs away from her new home.

The message of the movie is that we require all of our emotions, not just the so-called positive ones. We soon realize that Joy's tendency to ignore and suppress Sadness is actually getting in the way of them finding their way home. It seems like things work pretty badly when just one of the emotions takes charge, and much better when they all work together through being equally valued.

Existential therapist Emmy Van Deurzen provides a useful explanation for why trying to shut down or eradicate some emotions is a bad idea.[2] She imagines all of the emotions on a wheel which we travel round all of the time, moving from "high" feelings like joy and pride, through anger and fear to low feelings like sadness, and then up the other side through envy and hope, to joy again (see Figure 5.2).

Emmy Van Deurzen says that we need to be able to experience all of the emotions in order to go around the wheel freely like this. If there are emotions which we shut down or avoid then we're likely to get stuck in certain places. Paradoxically if we disallow one emotion—like sadness—we're likely to become stuck and find that we stop experiencing joy much too. If we lose the capacity

---

2   Van Deurzen, E. (2008) *Psychotherapy and the Quest for Happiness.* London: Sage.

to experience some of the emotions entirely we risk falling into depression and all of our emotions becoming shut off.

Figure 5.2: Compass of emotions

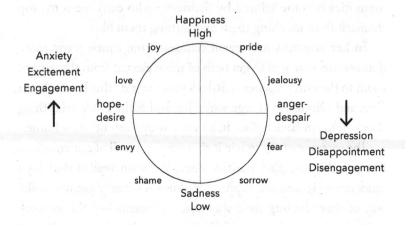

It may not be that we always move in the same direction on the wheel, or that certain emotions always follow others. Indeed we can often experience seemingly opposing emotions at the same time (joy and sadness, anger and hope, fear and determination). Existential therapists regard all feelings as sensible responses that have something to tell us, as long as we're up for listening to them.

Another risk of trying not to feel certain emotions is—as MJ found—that trying to avoid a "negative" feeling can mean that you experience many more difficult feelings than if you had managed to experience the first feeling. Buddhists refer to this as the "second arrow". It's like we're hit by one arrow (the feeling) and then another one (the feeling about the feeling). For example, if we've been taught to protect other people from our anger, any angry feelings are likely to be followed by a wave of guilt or shame.

Another issue is emotional gaslighting. If we try to shut down or repress our own feelings then other people often pick up on them regardless, especially those who we're close to and/

or those who have learnt to be hypervigilant to others' emotional states due to experiences of trauma. For example, MJ often felt the feelings that their parents were not expressing, and then felt self-doubting and crazy when the presence of those feelings was denied, as well as responsible and self-blaming for having these unacceptable reactions. We may explicitly or implicitly punish the other person for expressing the feelings that we're trying to escape from or eradicate, which can be extremely tough and confusing for them.

How can we stay with all of our feelings?

So what can we do if—as most of us have—we've learnt to welcome some emotional states and to shut off or distance from others? The answer that many therapies and spiritualities have come up with over the years is to practice staying with feelings. Each time we stay with a feeling, rather than trying to fight it or run from it, we give ourselves the important message that all feelings are valid and acceptable, and we'll probably find that we learn a lot of useful information about ourselves as well.

More evidence that experiencing all our emotions is important comes from humanistic therapist Eugene Gendlin. He studied the differences between people whose lives improved after counselling, and those who didn't feel any better. Listening to many recordings of therapy sessions he noticed that the clients who therapy helped did something that the other clients didn't do. This was a kind of checking in where they slowed down, tuned in to themselves, and reported what they were experiencing, often explaining how they were feeling in their bodies, and trying to find the best words to describe their emotional experience.

Gendlin went on to develop *focusing* as a practice for people to learn how to stay with their feelings like this. It involves tuning into the felt sense of the emotion in your body, and going through a process of finding the best words, images, and/or metaphors to capture it. *Mindfulness* also includes similar practices, often based on Buddhist spirituality. For example, Chöd practice has been adapted for Western cultures by writers such as Lama Tsultrim Allione. Like focusing, this involves tuning into the experience of an emotion in your body, but then you visualize it as a demon sitting opposite you. You ask the demon what it wants, what it needs, and how it would feel if it got what it needed. Then you inhabit the demon in order to feel what that is like and answer those questions. Back in yourself you imagine dissolving into whatever feeling the demon mentioned and feeding the demon with that feeling. You then notice what happens.

We've included focusing and demon-feeding practices in the Further Resources at the end of the chapter in case you fancy trying those out. They work particularly well if you like bodily and/or visual practices. Meanwhile here is a simpler practice for staying with feelings from Pema Chödrön[3] to try out.

> *Thought experiment: FEAR practice*
> *Try this practice for a feeling that is around for you at the moment—whether you'd describe it as positive or negative:*
> *Find the feeling in your body.*
> *Embrace it (instead of trying to get rid of it, or distracting yourself from it).*
> *Allow thoughts about it to dissolve, and abide with the feeling.*
> *Remember all of the other people who feel, and have felt, this way.*

Pema talks about how we often get caught up in a *storyline* about feelings. For example, "Oh no, I'm feeling low, what's going on? Maybe I'm falling into depression. What's wrong with me?

---

3   Chödrön, P. *Walking the Walk: Putting the Teachings into Practice When It Matters Most* [CD]. Louisville: Sounds True.

Everything's going well—I shouldn't feel depressed. It's stupid to be feeling like this. I'm so fed up with myself. Other people have far worse things going on than I do. Etc. etc. etc." *Allowing* the thoughts to dissolve is about letting go of these storylines and just remaining with the actual feeling: its texture, strength, color, where you feel it in your body, sensation, and so on.

It can also be really helpful to *remember* to use tough feelings as a way of connecting with all the other people who are feeling this way. This turns you outwards towards the world, develops compassion, and can leave you feeling less alone.

In her writings Pema suggests making staying with uncomfortable feelings into a lifelong practice, arguing that this is the path to being more open to life and to relationships with others. When we shut down and try to protect ourselves from difficult feelings we distance from both ourselves and each other.

Staying with other people's feelings

Staying with other people's feelings is just as important as staying with our own, and cultivating the capacity to stay with our own feelings can help a lot with this. However, another binary comes into play when we relate to other people's feelings, which is whether we regard ourselves—or them—as responsible for their feelings. We think of this as "you made me feel…" versus "own your feelings".

A common way of understanding feelings is that we cause other people to feel things and that we should take complete responsibility for this. People often say "you made me feel angry/scared/good/happy, etc." and we rarely question the truth of this. This often means that if somebody expresses a feeling in relation to something that we are involved with we feel entirely responsible for them having that feeling. If we're also trying to ensure that people only have "positive" feelings, and no "negative" ones, we may feel wonderful if those around us are happy (to the extent that we put pressure on them to be so) and distraught if they are not.

Perhaps in response to the problems with this common way of viewing other people's feelings, several authors on topics like assertiveness, relationships, and conflict management put forward the alternative approach that we are not at all responsible for other people's emotions. The idea of owning our emotions suggests that nobody makes us feel anything except ourselves. We can choose how to make sense of other people's behaviors, and thus we are in control of any emotional response we have: it belongs to us. An extension of this idea is that we would certainly reject any accusation that we had made anybody feel anything.

Both of these approaches treat people as if they are entirely separate selves. Feeling responsible for others' feelings treats people as if we were isolated billiard balls, bashing up against each other and causing effects when we do so. Owning our emotions suggests that we are entirely separate individuals and capable of determining our own feelings regardless of what happens in the world around us. As we've seen through this book, we're better understood as interdependent, interconnected beings.

Also neither of the two approaches are very useful. When we subscribe to the "making people feel…" view we often become overwhelmed with self-blame and guilt when somebody expresses displeasure with something that we have done, or even when they just express unhappiness in our presence. Imagine you go to a friend's house and break their favorite vase. If you then become deeply and visibly distressed about what you've done, the other person may end up comforting you and pushing aside their own feelings of loss. It's like when a white person says or does something that's marginalizing or excluding to people of color. When this is pointed out they often become so overwhelmed by the horror that they might be perceived as racist that others around them end up looking after them rather than the people who have been adversely impacted by their comments or actions.

On the other hand, the "owning emotions" view can easily be used as an excuse for denying other people's feelings. For example, when we make changes in our lives which are tough on a partner or friend because we can't offer what we used to offer to them, the temptation is strong to blame the other person for any tough feelings that they have about the situation, to offer endless excuses and justifications for what we've done, and/or to claim that it's unreasonable for them to feel how they feel. This way of behaving is also common in those kinds of race conversations: people say that it wasn't intentional on their part, or that the other person is being over-sensitive, dramatic, or derailing.

An alternative approach between taking all or none of the responsibility is to recognize our mutuality and interconnectedness with other people in a way which appreciates how we, together, build our realities, and to treat emotions as *relational*. Thus what we say and do can open things up or close things down, for others, and vice versa, in an ongoing process over time.

For example, if we have made a change that alters another person's life in ways that are painful to them, we can listen to, and respect, their feelings while still holding on to the fact it was something we needed to do (instead of dismissing their feelings, or going back on our decision and then resenting them for it). If we have spoken or acted in ways that marginalize or exclude others we can own up to that without beating ourselves up for our (inevitable) limitations and imperfections, and hopefully commit to being more aware next time (rather than becoming so burnt out by the experience that there is no next time).

We'll come back to this way of approaching things in the final chapter of the book. For now let's look at one final emotions binary: that between madness and sanity.

5.4 The mad/sane binary

As we've mentioned throughout this chapter, we've both experienced mental health struggles of various kinds throughout our lives. Earlier we spoke about the ways CPTSD can leave Alex struggling with intense feelings and self-critical thoughts. After their early experiences of bullying and feeling unacceptable at home, MJ too has experienced a high level of self-critical background noise: thoughts that they've done something terribly wrong, or that they will do, or that there's something wrong with them. This has seen them alternating between anxious, people-pleasing mode and dropping into depression and self-loathing. Beginning to loosen their non-binary thinking about themself has helped with this. We'll come back to that in the next chapter.

Despite these experiences we've both always been critical around standard approaches to mental health, particularly some of the labels that are often used for people with such experiences and the "us and them" way mental health systems often divide the professionals (us—well) from the patients or clients (them—ill).

We've probably both ticked the boxes for several of the recognized "psychiatric disorders" in our time, but we don't feel comfortable identifying with some of these, particularly those that locate issues as internal "personality disorders" rather than stressing the external causes, as CPTSD endeavors to do. Equally though, we wouldn't feel comfortable identifying as sane, mentally well, or psychologically healthy. As with so much in life, we feel that the binary—in this case between "mad" and "sane"—is actually part of the problem.

> ### Reflection point: Mental health
> Would you describe yourself as having any mental health issues? If so, how do you know that this is the case? What words do you use to label these—if any—and why? If you wouldn't describe yourself as having any mental health struggles do you see yourself as "sane" or "mentally well"? If so what does this mean to you and how do you know to see yourself in this way?

Mental health/illness

The mad/sane binary is present in all of the mainstream messages that we receive about mental health. For example, high profile campaigns to end mental health discrimination often center around one, apparently game-changing, statistic, such as one in four people having a mental health problem. Celebrities like Stephen Fry and Ruby Wax have used the figure to speak bravely and openly about their experience of mental ill health, but the danger of that statistic is that it suggests that 75 percent of the population don't experience any mental health problems. Rather than seeing mental health as a spectrum which we might all move up and down over the course of our lives, we're forced to stake our identity on one or other side of a strict dividing line:

Either… I have a mental health problem—I need help—it's not my fault.

Or… I don't have a mental health problem—I don't get help—it is my fault.

In this way we're placed in a double bind, because accepting one side inevitably involves denying the other, and neither side promises a great outcome. If we're seen as having a mental health problem we may well feel utterly disempowered, as if there's nothing that we can do to improve our situation. If we're seen as not having a mental health problem we might feel like we can't admit to having any problems or get any support because we're completely responsible for our own happiness and wellbeing. The responsibility either rests entirely with other people, or entirely with ourselves, and either way that puts us in an untenable position.

Linked to this is the fact that both sides of the binary internalize suffering, seeing it as a purely individual thing, rather than a symptom of wider social issues. We're forced to view mental health problems as inborn, either caused by illness (perhaps a genetic vulnerability and/or brain chemistry issue) or by a personal deficiency (such as bad habits, faulty thinking, or lack of moral fiber). This can be very damaging because—as we've already mentioned several times through this book—there's strong evidence that all our human experiences are biopsychosocial: a complex interaction between the world around us, our personal experiences of it, and our bodies and brains, with all of those aspects influencing the others. We risk doing further damage to ourselves when we attempt to change our individual experience without recognizing the role of social injustice and/or cultural messages in our suffering.

Whichever side of the biology/personal responsibility binary a person is seen as falling on, there's little or no acknowledgement of the involvement of wider cultural messages and societal structures in their suffering.

Social suffering

It's clear that structural oppression and social injustice have a major role in mental health struggles because we see far higher rates of such difficulties in groups who are marginalized. One recent UK study found that women were 40 percent more likely to develop anxiety and depression than men, another found that LGB people are twice as likely to be suicidal as straight people, and a further one that people of color are six times more likely than white people to be admitted as in patients in mental health services. We need to recognize the role of intersecting marginalizations in mental health struggles, and the ways in which social experiences such as poverty, discrimination, and the experience of trauma are highly related to psychological distress.

We also live in a culture which encourages the very kind of self-critical thinking that's a feature of all the most common mental health problems. The French philosopher Michel Foucault famously used the analogy of the panopticon prison for our culture. In this prison there's a single guard sitting at the top of a central tower in the middle who is able to see into all of the prison cells. Prisoners end up monitoring their own behavior all of the time, just in case they might currently be being watched.

Foucault argued that our culture works in this way through all of the pressure we're under to self-improve, and to present a positive, successful self to the world. We're made to feel fear that we might be lacking or failing in some way, and we're sold products which claim to help us to allay those fears. Makeover shows, self-help books, and beauty products are some of the more obvious examples. Social media also encourages us to maintain the illusion of perfection online, leading to endless rounds of self-evaluation and comparison.

In a world where so many of us are struggling with very real social problems, it's vitally important to acknowledge the cultural context we're in and to resist individualizing our suffering. The mad/sane binary is very effective in preventing challenges to toxic policies and practices because people are not aware of the social context of their struggles, and because there is a fear that if you do speak out you will be dismissed as "insane".

We can see this at play in the recent moves to regard un-employment as a psychological problem and the insistence that those claiming benefits undergo cognitive behavioral therapy. The responsibility is placed on the individual rather than on wider societal problems, and resources are focused on psychological change rather than addressing economic inequalities. There's a high risk that people are left in the same damaging situation, but with an even greater tendency to blame themselves for it.

A sane response to a mad world?

The psychotherapist Winnicott famously said, of depression:

> The capacity to become depressed...is something that is not inborn
> nor is it an illness; it comes as an achievement of healthy emotional
> growth...the fact is that life itself is difficult...probably the greatest
> suffering in the human world is the suffering of normal or healthy or
> mature persons.[4]

Perhaps we would do well to view the depression, anxiety, and other mental health struggles that most of us grapple with at some point as a sane response to an insane world. This would shift the emphasis for change away from the individual and towards the wider societal structures and cultural messages around us.

Linking this back to "positive" and "negative" emotions, in her book, *The Promise of Happiness*, Sara Ahmed talks about the ways in which happiness may be more available to some rather than others, often those who can more easily conform to the "norm" and can achieve what our culture deems as "success" or "happily-ever-after". She suggests that we require "feminist killjoys", "melancholy

---

4   Winnicott, D.W. (1988) *Human Nature*. London: Free Association Books, p.149.

migrants", and "unhappy queers" to speak from "negative emotions" if we are to reach a more equal society where pleasure isn't always found at the expense of others or by conforming to problematic power hierarchies which value some bodies, lives, and labour more highly than others, both financially and otherwise (see Chapter 4).

However, mental health systems can be very resistant to such views. In *Users and Abusers of Psychiatry*, Lucy Johnstone suggests that it is very tempting for mental health practitioners to treat clients or patients in an "us (well) and them (ill)" way because of how invested they are in the current system. There's the danger that, without such clear splits, their job security would be at risk. Also they would lose the sense of expertise and professional power that they have if, for example, there was a de-medicalizing of distress or a de-professionalization of support for people who were struggling. There is a danger, more widely, that those who have an investment in being seen as sane, in control, and professional, require a comparison group of those who aren't. This may play out in mental health systems, in families and other groups, and in society at large. Mad pride and communities of survivors of mental health systems endeavor to address these issues in their work.

We know that it has helped us a lot to recognize the social and cultural aspects of our struggles. It can be a huge relief to allow the weight of total responsibility to lift and to recognize the role of internalized self-criticism and the trauma we've experienced through marginalization in our experiences.

This acknowledgement also allows us to engage critically with the mad/sane binary: resisting the sense that we're completely responsible for our difficulties and the sense that we have no capacity at all to help ourselves. In this way we can all cultivate a kinder relationship with ourselves, on the one hand, and feel more of a sense of kinship with all of the others who are in the same cultural boat, on the other. Such connections enable the possibility for collective resistance and for social activism, which feel like a much better focus for our energy than continually trying to change ourselves.

Multiple experiences: Mental health labels

Where does this leave us with diagnosis? We could resist any form of diagnosis as a way of individualizing and medicalizing problems, which are actually highly social and cultural, and for reinforcing mad/sane binaries. However, diagnoses can be incredibly helpful for people too. Rather than trying to come to a binary good/bad decision on diagnosis, perhaps it's more useful to ask what it opens up and closes down for people, being mindful that it can often do both. Here are some examples of people's differing relationships to mental health labels.

- "Initially I was diagnosed with borderline personality disorder (BPD). That felt terrible to me. Like there was something wrong with my whole character, and the negativity around BPD made me feel like I was stuck there forever and could never have a good relationship. The shift to a diagnosis of CPTSD was a huge deal for me, because it put the emphasis on the trauma I'd experienced and the systems responsible for that. It also felt like there was a lot more clarity about things that could help when your trauma got triggered."
- "When I'm having a hard time in life I watch a lot of porn. My partner thought I might be a sex addict. When I looked it up online it felt good to think that there might be an explanation for what I was going through, rather than it being my fault, and that there were a community of people who experienced this too who might support me. However, I struggled with the idea that I had to accept I

am an addict and will always be one. Some of the other people's experiences were pretty different to mine. Also, it's more the way that I engage with porn that I'd like to change. I still think that watching ethically produced porn can be a great part of my sex life."

- "I hate the fact that trans experiences are still classed as psychiatric disorders. It's completely inappropriate; we should just embrace the full range of gender diversity as equally valid, and provide medical assistance to those who need it to feel more comfortable in themselves regardless of whether they are trans or cis. However I will admit that when I sat down with my psychiatrist—who is an awesome ally—to get my referral for surgery, it did feel affirming to have a moment of being seen and recognized as trans, even if it did come attached to a problematic psychiatric label."

- "I deliberately embrace the label 'mad' to challenge the stigma attached to mental illness and to express my rage against psychiatric systems. As a psychiatric survivor I want to see an end to the institutional violence, human rights violations, and other forms of oppression which people who are psychiatrically assigned are subjected to."

- "I resisted the term 'depression' for a long time because I didn't want to believe there was anything wrong with me, but now I use it because it is the best way to explain what I'm going through to other people in a way they understand, and I need a label in order to take sick leave from work when I'm struggling. Similarly I resisted medication because I thought I should be able to sort it out for myself. Now I do find that antidepressants are helpful, alongside talking therapy, and doing activism around mental health. I'm glad I allowed myself to do something that lifted my mood; it was an act of kindness."

This idea of asking what things open up and what they close down leads us nicely to the final chapter of the book, which is on non-binary thinking. Why do we get stuck in binary thinking across all the topics we've covered in this book—and more? And how might we shift that if we want to think differently about things?

Further Resources

You can read more about emotions and mental health from similar perspectives to the ones we explore here in the following books:

- Ahmed, S. (2010) *The Promise of Happiness*. Durham, NC: Duke University Press. (feministkilljoys.com)
- Bentall, R.P. (2010) *Doctoring the Mind: Why Psychiatric Treatments Fail*. London: Penguin.
- Chödrön, P. (2010) *The Wisdom of No Escape: And the Path of Loving-Kindness*. Boulder, CO: Shambhala Publications. (pemachodronfoundation.org)
- Cornell, A.W. (2000) *The Power of Focusing*. Thinking Allowed Productions. (www.focusing.org, www.focusing.org.uk)
- DeGruy, J. (2005) *Post Traumatic Slave Syndrome: America's Legacy of Enduring Injury and Healing*. Milwaukie, OR: Uptone Press.
- Fredman, G. (2004) *Transforming Emotion: Conversations in Counselling and Psychotherapy*. London: Whurr. (http://www.taosinstitute.net/glenda-fredman-phd)
- Johnstone, L. (2000) *Users and Abusers of Psychiatry: A Critical Look at Psychiatric Practice*. Hove: Routledge.
- Kain, K.L. and Terrell, S.J. (2018) *Nurturing Resilience: Helping Clients Move Forward from Developmental Trauma. An Integrative Somatic Approach*. Berkeley, CA: North Atlantic Books.

- Magid, B. (2008) *Ending the Pursuit of Happiness.* Boston, MA: Wisdom Publications.
- Menakem, R. (2017) *My Grandmother's Hands: Racialized Trauma and the Pathway to Mending Our Hearts and Bodies.* Las Vegas, NV: Central Recovery Press.
- Metzl, J.M. (2010) *The Protest Psychosis: How Schizophrenia Became a Black Disease.* Boston, MA: Beacon Press.
- Van Deurzen, E. (2009) *Psychotherapy and the Quest for Happiness.* London: Sage. (www.emmyvandeurzen.com)

To apply these ideas more to your life, check these out:

- Allione, Lama T. (2017) *How to feed your demons.* Available from: lionsroar.com/how-to-practice-feeding-your-demons
- Barker, M-J. (2015) *Social mindfulness.* Available from: rewriting-the-rules.com/zines.
- Barker, M-J. (2016) *Staying with feelings zine.* Available from: rewriting-the-rules.com/zines.
- Barker, M-J. and Hancock, J. (2018) *Staying with feelings in relationship podcast.* Available from: megjohnandjustin.com/relationships/staying-with-feelings-in-relationships.

Many thanks to Ladybeard Magazine for publishing an early version of the final section of this chapter.

CHAPTER 6
Thinking

All the way through this book we've been exploring how thinking about things in binary ways is unhelpful. We've discussed how binary thinking around sex erases bisexual identities and suggests that some experiences of sex are more "proper" or "normal" than others, making it hard for people to tune into their sexual experiences and to behave consensually. We've explored how binary thinking around gender has been a vital feature in the history of patriarchal oppression, and how it marginalizes trans and non-binary experiences, and leaves people feeling they have to cling tightly to rigid gender roles that are often painful and unhelpful. We've suggested that people also think in binary ways around relationships: dividing certain types of relationships from others (e.g. monogamous/non-monogamous, lovers/friends) and privileging one side over the other. In the chapter on bodies we explored how bodies are also divided into hierarchical binaries in ways that legitimize the treatment of some bodies as more valuable than others. And in the last chapter we considered mind/body, emotional/rational, and positive/negative binary thinking as underlying a lot of human distress.

In this final chapter of the book we want to broaden out the theme of non-binary thinking to ask—first—how binary thinking underlies our struggles more widely than the examples we've already explored and—second—how we might go about thinking in different ways. We revisit the involvement of non-binary thinking in aspects of human suffering such as conflict and mental health difficulties and then ask: if we buy the argument that binary thinking is unhelpful across many domains of human experience— what might non-binary thinking look like? We offer a range of practices which may help us to think in more non-binary, both/and, or uncertain ways, drawing on Buddhist mindfulness, Paganism, and queer theory, among other approaches.

6.1 The role of binary thinking in debates and conflict

In this section we'll explore the role of binary thinking in conflict. The first step to conflict frequently—if not always—involves framing something as a debate between two positions, one of which is assumed to be "right" and the other "wrong". We then "pick a side", polarizing into "us and them" where "we" are right and therefore good and "they" are wrong and therefore bad. This often legitimizes increasingly unacceptable behavior towards "them" because if we are on the side of the "right", then we are justified in doing whatever we have to in order to win (rather than lose). Also, remaining haunted by the idea that we might actually be on the other side of the binary (wrong or bad) can make us fight all the harder to defend our position.

Framing things as debates

Generally speaking, when people discuss contentious issues, they polarize into "for" or "against". The underlying question driving the debate is whether this thing we're talking about is a good thing or a bad thing: whether it helps people or harms people, or sometimes even whether it even exists or not. It's so hard not to slip into these binary ways of thinking and talking about issues because they're so entrenched in our culture. The framing of everything as a debate is so taken-for-granted in mainstream media that journalists and programme-makers often struggle to understand when we suggest to them that finding some people from "the other side" to "balance the debate" isn't a great approach.

Debate framing is a pretty dangerous way of addressing things because it leads to a lot of muddled thinking, as well as the tendency to divide people into "us" and "them" on the basis of their positions. And, of course, "we" are the enlightened, rational people with all the objective knowledge on the subject, and "they" are the irrational, biased folks basing their opinions on pseudoscience and opinion. This kind of polarization prevents us from listening openly to others and potentially finding our way to more complex and nuanced understandings and smart ways of engaging with the issues that face us.

Framing things as debates also often legitimizes problematic views. For example, MJ remembers being invited to take part in a debate on whether bisexuality exists. The people hosting the debate thought they were doing something open and positive by holding a debate on this often-invisible topic and demonstrating that they wanted to hear "both sides". However, on a topic where there is really no question—obviously people exist in the world who are attracted to more than one gender—framing it as a debate actually opens up the possibility that there is something to question, when of course there isn't. Given the already existing suspicion around bisexual existence, this is supremely unhelpful.

Climate change is another useful example where media people often assume that the best way to tackle the topic—as with pretty much any topic they address—is to bring people from "both sides" into debate. Again this legitimizes the very small number of people who are invested in denying climate change, potentially making it easier for the rest of us to shrug off the dangers of our behaviors—and those of big businesses and institutions—because climate change is "still up for debate".

Polarizing

When we frame everything as a debate, then everything becomes a sort of competition. We're used to debates being "won or lost" (another binary!), or being resolved by "agreeing to disagree", which, as we discuss later, is not only unsatisfactory, but downright dangerous for marginalized communities. At the heart of this type of framework is another foundational binary: us/them. We call this a foundational binary because it's literally part of the foundations of most binary thinking leading to conflict and injustice, as discussed in Chapter 3.

As Nat Titman[1] points out, framing things as polarized debates is a political strategy which can be highly dangerous:

> A quintessential part of propaganda tactics used by extremist hate and terror groups is to cause and amplify polarization in society to force people into opposing extremes. So how to oppose racist hate groups with the full strength deserved without playing into the

1   Personal communication.

polarization narratives these groups want to create and misuse to pull others into their hateful ideology and isolate them from moderating influences?

We're currently seeing these tactics being used in various countries on a global level as we witness a resurgence in white supremacy and other forms of extremism.

These tactics can be often purveyed under the banner of free speech, something that many of us would agree is a good thing. People who are engaged in debating other people's existence or legitimacy often invoke free speech to protect their right to say what they want. This seems to have given rise to the false binary of free speech advocates versus social justice warriors, with the latter being seen as people who censor "free" or "unpopular" "thinkers". This is, however, a false binary given that it's based on the conflation of opinions with facts and the right for people to exist safely in the world. For example, whether I like pineapple on pizza, or how much tax we should collect can be matters of opinion. On the other hand, trans people's existence and the number of Black and Brown, Indigenous, trans, and disabled people being discriminated against, harassed, and murdered are facts. When opinion and facts become equivalent, and when people's lives become a matter of debate, that's when we start to get into the lethal waters of fascist rhetoric masquerading as free speech.

As Whitney Phillips[2] puts it:

What do you do, for example, when calls for freedom of expression undermine the objective of cultivating free expression, particularly

---

2   See https://motherboard.vice.com/en_us/article/vb73zm/berkeley-doesnt-have-to-choose-between-social-justice-and-free-speech

when considering explicitly racist, misogynist, and other bigoted forms of expression, which silence or at least attempt to pathologize historically marginalized perspectives? Who gets to draw the line between democratically healthy and democratically toxic speech? Who gets to decide who speaks?

We've felt the problems with debate framing very keenly ourselves in the "debates" around trans experience. Many people assume these conversations must be reasonable because why would you not want an open debate? However, as Samantha Allen rightly points out in her article,[3] "both sides journalism" fails when we're talking about a debate over whether an already marginalized group of people exist or deserve rights at all.

When things are framed as a debate we need to ask ourselves:

1. Are both "sides" of this debate equally valid, for example according to the research evidence in this area?
2. Do both "sides" of this debate have equal power, or is one already positioned as way more powerful than the other?
3. Whose voices are heard in these debates and whose are not?
4. Are these the only positions on this topic that are available, or might there be many other perspectives which are obscured by this debate framing?
5. Who stands to gain from framing this as a debate in this way?

For example, in the UK the "trans debate" is often framed as trans-exclusionary feminists versus trans feminists. This fits into a

---

3   See www.thedailybeast.com/how-both-sides-journalism-is-failing-transgender-people

much older media pattern of pitching different feminists against each other in "cat fights" which deligitimizes feminism as a whole, reinforces stereotypes of women as emotional, and focuses feminist energy on internal battles and away from the broader—essential— fight to dismantle patriarchy.

Reflection point: Your experience of debates

Think about debates which are close to your heart that play out over mainstream and social media. How does the tendency to frame it as a debate and to polarize into right/ wrong positions lead to problems in this area? For example, you might think about debates around veganism and the way these do or do not capture complexities of ethical food consumption, or debates around immigration, sex work, abortion, or other matters.

When we frame everything as a debate, we can also try to mask or distance ourselves from conflict. In dominant culture, conflict can be viewed as "negative" and to be avoided, in favor of "harmony and unity". However, conflict can be understood as a fundamental part of intimacy (see Chapter 3). It is often through conflict that we can get to know each other better, if we can dare to become vulnerable with one another. When we try to move away from conflict at all costs, we can become stuck on our side of the fence, by digging our heels in, thinking we "have to be right" as "being wrong" equals "being bad" and is, as such, intolerable. There is more on how this type of thinking can inflict suffering on ourselves and others in the next section. Before we move on though, let's take a moment to think about our relationship with conflict and where we might have learned how to engage in it, or not.

Thought experiment: Your relationship with conflict

For this thought experiment, you might need a pencil/pen and paper, or you can just use your imagination instead. We invite you to think of your life as if it were a river. The river can have tributaries/ affluent streams, if you want, but it does not need to. Each bend of the river is a significant moment, encounter, person, movie, book, insight that has defined you in some way. Before drawing, or imagining, your river, think of what you know about conflict. What is your relationship with conflict? Where have you learned about conflict? From whom? Now as you draw or imagine your river, each bend represents a pivotal moment, encounter, person, movie, book, insight that has defined how you have come to understand and engage in conflict today. You may want to annotate each bend with keywords or illustrations to remind you what they represent.

Once you have drawn or imagined your river, take a moment to revisit it and reflect on how those different bends have impacted you and others. What is your relationship with this river? How has it changed over time? If you want to keep using this metaphor, for example, were you swimming in the river, sitting by its shore, canoeing in it, drowning in it, or merrily floating? What was the weather like in different parts of your journey?

Once you have done this, we invite you to revisit the river one more time. What did each bend teach you about us/them? Is this part of your thinking? Is it not? How has it served your survival to know who you are and who "others" are? How has it hindered possibilities for connection? What has each bend opened up or closed down? Try to do this with as much curiosity and non-judgment as you can in this moment. It can be a lot to take in so take care of yourself as you do this.

6.2 The role of binary thinking in suffering

We've talked in the previous section of how we might want to distance ourselves from conflict. You might have even learned a little bit more of how this works for you in the above thought experiment. One of the things that might feel challenging is to experience emotions associated with conflict, such as fear and anger.

When we're in conflict with another person, we might be afraid of losing the relationship with that person in our life. We might also be afraid of losing our jobs, our families, faith communities, or identity communities in which we experience a sense of belonging. The idea of being in conflict can, therefore, become unbearable as it can become overcoupled—that is so deeply entwined that we can no longer see the difference—with the idea of loss.

When we're in conflict we might also feel angry, in whatever nuance of anger we're able to tolerate. This might manifest as irritation, detachment, or blaming for example. In dominant culture, anger is often depicted as a negative emotion and as being expressed in a "hot-headed" manner. For example, in the movie *Inside Out*—which we spoke about in the previous chapter—Anger is portrayed as literally having flames coming out of their head. However anger can also be cold. It can be the way we push away from someone and cut them off by not sharing where we're at. Anger can look like a wall of ice between us and others.

Both anger and loss are things that we might try to avoid as humans and that get a "bad press" in dominant culture. Nevertheless, we might find ourselves in a paradox: while we're hypervigilant about our fear of conflict, and the accompanying potentiality of anger and loss, we're not paying as much attention to the suffering that is caused by trying to avoid them.

What we pay attention to matters

One of the theories that explains why we might be prone to paying attention to our fear of conflict, and not to the suffering caused by trying to avoid this, is the idea of negativity bias. According to this theory, it's more likely that people will pay attention to negative states and be more impacted by them. Some people think this trait is connected to the development of our survival senses: we need to pay more attention to things that might be dangerous to us, since they can be harmful.

This can mean, however, that everything could look dangerous and potentially harmful. When this happens, trust—both with others and ourselves—becomes difficult. We have talked about CPTSD and developmental trauma in Chapter 5 already. When we hold trauma—that is the impact of what has happened to us—in our bodies, our thinking is impacted too, as it's often no longer driven by the prefrontal cortex, but rather from other parts of our brain, starting from the amygdala and then impacting our nervous system in particular ways.

The tricky thing is that the amygdala was not designed for discernment and it cannot recognize whether we're experiencing an actual threat, or if responses are being triggered in our body due to past trauma, including cultural, social, historical, and intergenerational trauma. Conflict then becomes even more terrifying. We might not trust ourselves to know the difference between healthy aggression and boundary setting and inappropriate anger being unleashed on us—or by us.

We've already touched on how when we live with CPTSD, and especially with developmental trauma, we might become trapped in polarized thinking. We might feel there is only this way or that way, and no other possibility when we find ourselves in conflict situations. This type of thinking can increase our suffering even more, leading us into a vicious circle of pain, which might seem inescapable. We might also find ourselves isolated, or isolating, and disconnected, or using substances or activities to numb and/or manage our pain.

Trauma and suffering

One of the most insidious things about trauma is that it's not about the "bad thing(s)" that happened to us but rather how they have impacted us, and how they can become stuck in us, held in our very being, and leading us to ongoing suffering. One of the ways in which we can suffer is the polarized thinking mentioned. We start to think of ourselves and others as "good" or "bad", "victims" or "perpetrators", as being a "success" or a "failure". We are then stuck in all/nothing thinking where we're both too much and not enough.

We're never good enough but the idea of being bad is intolerable. Trying to compensate for being "not enough" we can easily tip into feeling that we're "too much" for others to tolerate us. We become hypervigilant and tend to experience forms of perfectionism. Something has to be perfect or is not worth doing, for example. Mistakes become intolerable as they are now signs of our—or other people's—lack of worth. We simply stop giving ourselves and others permission to be fully human. We end up living in terror of everything and everyone around us but, above all, of our own selves.

However, because the idea that we might be "truly bad" is intolerable, we often find ourselves blaming others in conflict situations. If we cannot be "bad" or "perpetrators", then someone else needs to be. We also start conflating behaviors with people. Here we're not denying that there are terrible behaviors and acts that people commit, but we're not prepared to turn others into monsters either, even though we admit there can be comfort in othering those who hurt us, since this is often the only way we can let ourselves express appropriate anger towards them.

The problem, when we do this, is that we become dogmatic in our beliefs and dogma often leads to more suffering. We start to lose sight of multiversality, that is the view that there are multiple realities that exist, and our world becomes narrower and narrower. It's not just other people then who now need to get through our narrow world view, but also ourselves. We have less and less space to be fully human, to make mistakes, and to learn. We become increasingly judgmental of ourselves, our thinking becomes rigid, and our standards are often impossible to attain.

This means that we also end up hiding our authentic selves from others, given that the danger is that we will be found out to be whatever we're most afraid of being. As we hide ourselves from others, we're then not as capable of genuine ventral vagal connection (another part of our nervous system, which lives in our gut), which is essential to our wellbeing. This means that we cannot fully relax into intimacy with ourselves, others, and the world around us, and we suffer from this lack of fundamental connection. We're now living in a constant state of stress and hypervigilance. Basically, we can never let our guard down, no matter where we are or who we're with.

This is, of course, untenable. When we live in a state of constant stress, we cannot access creativity and play, which are essential to our mental health. We also find it difficult, if not impossible, to learn new things. Language learning, for example, includes a significant amount of play, as children developing language make up their own rules, play with existing rules, interact with others, and eventually learn a first language. Our lives become smaller and we cannot settle or often even sleep very well, or we might sleep too much.

We become trapped into our own selves and all the terrible things that might be in our mind because of the ways in which we have been hurt. As we cut ourselves off from the anger that we could not safely express towards the people who hurt us, we find that we have turned that anger towards ourselves in many other ways. As we cut ourselves off from the pain of potential loss, we find that we're more and more isolated, given that we are afraid of connecting vulnerably with others. Sadly, we also cannot see any other possibilities, any other choices, any other ways of being.

The good news, as we said in Chapter 5, is that we do have access to neuroplasticity and we do not need to stay stuck in pain. However, this is easier said than done, as we keep exploring in the rest of this section, before moving on to some more strategies to flex our non-binary thinking muscles.

Decisions

As with the wider cultural framing of debates which we covered in the first section of this chapter, when faced with a decision we often find ourselves assuming that there are two possible options: one of which is right and the other of which is wrong. Starting from this taken-for-granted assumption we can easily tie ourselves in knots trying to decide which is which. If we have experienced early and/or repeated traumatic events, we might find that these knots are even tighter.

What can be much more helpful is to question that foundational assumption. Are there only two options or might there be many we could consider which are in between those two or outside of them? Even considering the two options that we have on the table, might there be both positive and negative possibilities along both potential paths rather than one being all positive and one all negative? And might we further question our polarizing of positive and negative things here, recognizing that what we regard as positive is likely to contain some negatives and vice versa.

We might reflect on the times when things we have really wanted have come with unanticipated difficulties, and the times when things we've dreaded have been very useful in some ways.

Similarly when we consider anything in our lives: jobs, people, relationships, holidays, tasks, and so on we can notice our tendency to polarize. This job is either all good or all bad, meaning that I should stay or I should leave. This person I have met is either my kind of person entirely or not at all and I should pursue a relationship with them or close down that possibility. This label is one that I embrace or discard. What I've achieved is either a success or a failure and I should celebrate or berate myself accordingly. This group, or way of thinking, or set of ideas, is either an "us" thing or a "them" thing, and I therefore accept it or reject it.

Reflection point: Polarizing
Think for yourself about the last time you made a decision. How much did you have a sense of there being a "right" or "wrong" answer? Does this idea that we polarize in relation to things in our lives make sense to you? In what ways do you see it playing out in your own life?

Taoist and Buddhist perspectives on suffering
A Taoist parable demonstrates our tendency to view everything in terms of "good" and "bad" and the suffering this can cause:

> The situation…is like that of the wise Chinese farmer whose horse ran off. When his neighbour came to console him the farmer said, "Who knows what's good or bad?"

When his horse returned the next day with a herd of horses following her, the foolish neighbour came to congratulate him on his good fortune. "Who knows what's good or bad?" said the farmer.

Then, when the farmer's son broke his leg trying to ride one of the new horses, the foolish neighbour came to console him again. "Who knows what's good or bad?" said the farmer.

When the army passed through, conscripting men for the war, they passed over the farmer's son because of his broken leg. When the foolish man came to congratulate the farmer that his son would be spared, again the farmer said, "Who knows what's good or bad?"

When do we expect the story to end?

This links to the Buddhist take on suffering, which suggests that suffering lies—not in the events of life which are bound to be painful at time and wonderful at times—but in our responses to them whereby we try to cling on to the "positive" experiences and avoid or eradicate the "negative" ones: just as the neighbour wants to celebrate or commiserate.

According to Buddhists, craving is our desire to grasp hold of everything that we want (e.g. approval from others, material things, and good feelings) and to hurl away from ourselves everything that we don't want (e.g. disapproval, pain, and unhappiness). Martine Batchelor[4] uses the analogy of a precious object:

Let's imagine that I am holding an object made of gold. It is so precious and it is mine—I feel I must hold onto it. I grasp it, curling my fingers so as not to drop it, so that nobody can take it away

---

4   Batchelor, M. (2001) *Meditation for Life*. London: Frances Lincoln, p. 96.

from me. What happens after a while? Not only do my hand and arm get cramp but I cannot use my hand for anything else. When you grip something, you create tension and limit yourself.

Dropping the golden object is not the solution. Non-attachment means learning to relax to uncurl the fingers and gently open the hand. When my hand is wide open and there is no tension, the precious object can rest lightly on my palm. I can still value the object and take care of it; I can put it down and pick it up; I can use my hand for doing something else.

Perhaps this tendency to categorize everything in binary ways is grounded in such habitual patterns of grasping or hurling away. And because we are so used to approaching the world in this way, having done it all our lives, it becomes very difficult to do otherwise. Thus we—your authors—notice that only seconds after we've written about the problems with binary thinking here, we're trying to decide whether we've had a good or bad writing day on the basis of how productive we've been and then rushing to escape the "negative" feelings this results in!

Pema Chödrön lists four pairs of binaries that color our experience of the word: pleasure and pain, gain and loss, praise and blame, fame and disgrace. Those are the ones where we're always trying to ensure we get lots of the former and none of the latter. The former feel like good things to achieve, the latter make us feel like we must be terrible people. Pema suggests that we get hooked in these patterns of attachment and avoidance, which means that it is much harder when we do experience the "negative" things, and much less enjoyable when we experience the "positive" ones too, because we quickly cling rigidly to them. In the next section we'll start to explore practices from various therapeutic and spiritual approaches to relate differently to such binaries.

Slow down!

As you know by now, this is a good time to take a break, if you want. It can be really activating to talk about all these topics.

This time we would like to invite you to do something really kind for yourself. We would encourage you to choose something that is kind both in this moment and in the longer term for you. For example, Alex loves gluten but is intolerant. Eating a glutenous donut for them might feel kind in the present, but unkind to future Alex!

If you cannot think of anything, here are some examples. You might like to:

take a nap,

read a favorite poem,

listen to music,

dance,

take a walk,

smell a flower,

drink a cup of hot chocolate,

journal,

take a warm bath or shower,

look at cute animals on the Internet,

get a small task done that you have been putting off,

plan meeting up with a friend,

wrap yourself in your favorite blanket,

or simply pause and breathe.

Whatever kindness activity you choose, take your time enjoying it. Let yourself savor the feeling of having done something kind for yourself.

Then, when you're ready, carry on reading.

6.3 Alternatives to binary thinking

All through this book we've given you examples of alternatives to binary thinking, such as when we explored how we might understand our sexualities and genders differently if we considered them to be on a spectrum, or multiple spectrums; when we considered what a cultural moment—like the #MeToo movement—opened up and closed down; and when we thought about whether we could hold the paradox of things being both negative and positive simultaneously.

In this section we'll draw out four different—related—ways of thinking non-binary that you might find helpful to apply when you find yourself drawn into binary thinking.

Between and both/and

We've discussed in Chapter 4 how bodies defy binaries. We contain multitudes of complex experiences, including those that are liminal and fall in between the cracks of arbitrarily determined categories. It is not just our human animal bodies that defy binaries, so does Nature at large. There are so many ways in which both red bloods—that is animals—and green bloods—that is trees, plants, and vegetation—reproduce, for example! This does not mean that there aren't "opposites", because there are; it just means that there are more than only polarizing forces in the world.

First of all, there is all that can happen in between polarizing forces, when they exist. There is such a vast landscape of phenomena in between. Water can, for example, be liquid, solid, or gaseous. Within all three states there are several different manifestations. In liquid form water can be found in rivers, the sea, and ponds, but it can also fall from the sky as gentle rain or come down in sheets during a downpour. Solid water can be found on frozen lakes and glaciers, as well as fall as hail. Water can rise as vapor from our bodies and from the land when it comes into contact with heat.

If water can have such a range of manifestations—and we haven't even gone into depth about what happens when different elements are combined together—then surely we too have vaster landscapes and possibilities than binary thinking would have us believe. When we can see ourselves and everything around us as multidimensional, binary thinking becomes more and more challenging because there are more than just two axes, or two variables. We basically go from flat, two-dimensional cartoon characters, to three-dimensional—at least—complex beings, and so does everyone and everything else around us!

Whether you consider identities, experiences, and phenomena to be on a spectrum, or whether you conceptualize them as landscapes—both metaphors used throughout the book—we hope that you can start to see the possibilities of thinking in both/and ways as well as in between. What do we mean by both/and and in between thinking?

Both/and thinking can take various forms. For example, it can be applied to decision-making processes in business, it is used in narrative therapy approaches, and actors engaged in improvisational comedy often use a "yes, and" technique. Both/and requires us to move away from the rigid binary of either/or—which closes down possibilities—to consider a binary that opens up more possibilities. We can be both scared *and* do something. We can more fully embrace the many paradoxical feelings, experiences, and identities that most of us embody when we choose a both/and approach. We—your authors—can be both deeply impacted by transphobia and also rejoice in our trans identities. Things that seem to be at odds coexist all the time. Both/and thinking enables us to express this.

However, as always, there isn't just one simple solution. It is not enough to just embrace both/and and then all our problems will be solved (we wish!). In fact, even both/and thinking can be damaging. Many people who do not accept certain human experiences that are different from theirs can at times use both/and thinking in destructive ways. Some trans-exclusionary feminists, for example, would have us believe that we can both have gender essentialism—that is the idea that our genitals determine our gender identities, roles, and experiences—*and* have trans people live happily alongside and separately from cis people. By this point we hope you can see the faultlines in that type of thinking. Both/and can simply not be applied here, as gender essentialism already erases any possibility for openness and co-existence by being a dogmatic, exclusionary, and indeed binary theory. Once again, our discernment is vital so that we don't become caught in false arguments where only the illusion of openness and possibility is offered, when in reality all doors have already been closed and the one true path already chosen.

This is where between thinking can come in useful. What is the space between the both/and, where are the borders, and who is drawing them? Liminal space is often a space of dreams, creativity, and possibility. Think of the twilight of dusk or the emerging light of dawn. These are the spaces in between, the spaces where something is not one thing or another; it is not yet day, and yet it is no longer night. Between thinking is more nuanced and requires us to let go of easy categories. It's the place between breathing in and breathing out, where we can maybe pause and notice what we're about to open up and close down with our ways of thinking, being, and doing.

Reflection point: Going beyond either/or

Can you think of a recent time when you have felt stuck in an either/or situation? All you could think was that you had to do something, or the opposite. For example, stay or leave, rest or work. If you try to apply both/and thinking to

> this situation, does anything change and, if so, how does it
> change? If you already use both/and, and between, types of
> thinking in your life, what difference do they make?

Opening up/closing down

Let's return to the kinds of debates, conflicts, and decision-making where people polarize into "right" and "wrong", "good" and "bad". We saw earlier that when we polarize we often position other people in ways that push them also to extremes, rather than enabling them to connect with us in the messy complexity of it all, where they might be more able to see our point of view and vice versa. We've developed the following set of questions to work through these issues in a different—more non-binary—way:

1. What are we talking about here? How is it defined? Is it one thing or many? If it is many things then we need to separate them out and address each element separately.
2. What possibilities does this open up, and what does it close down? This is a more useful question than "is it good or bad?" because it recognizes that most things have the potential to be both. It also keeps our focus on the impact of whatever we're concerned about.
3. Given the first two answers, how might we creatively engage with this thing: finding an alternative to either completely embracing it (good) or attempting to eradicate it (bad)?

In their book, *The Psychology of Sex*, MJ uses this structure to explore some of the common "debates" around sex and sexuality. For example, it's a really useful way of unpacking the complexity of the "porn debates". The first point helps us to see that "porn" is not one thing, but rather a big umbrella which includes many materials that are designed to be arousing, including erotic fan fiction, mainstream porn magazines, feminist queer porn films, ancient erotic images, online clips that circulate, and more. It doesn't make sense to lump all these things together and ask whether they are "good" or "bad" for people or society. The second point reminds us that—like most things—porn (or even one of these kinds of porn) probably opens some stuff up, and closes some stuff down. For example, Alan McKee points out that young people get a lot of useful things from viewing porn (e.g. it helps them to learn about what they might enjoy, to communicate openly with partners about what they'd like to try, and to feel that sex can be pleasurable and should be joyful), but that it's also limited (e.g. because most porn doesn't include consent conversations, and gives an unrealistic idea about how bodies and sex work). This leads to point three, that perhaps instead of trying to eradicate porn—or argue that it's all wonderful when clearly it isn't—we could creatively engage, for example by providing great sex and relationships education which offers the things that are missing in porn; by developing forms of porn and erotica with consent at their heart; or by addressing the wider problematic social dynamics that are the reason that some porn is problematic (e.g. in terms of gender roles and the diversity of bodies included).

On their blog MJ also applies this same approach to the heated debates around trigger warnings. For point one they reflect that people mean many different things when they talk about "triggers". On both sides of the debate people focus on certain examples to make their point. For example, those on the "pro" side often highlight what seem to be incontrovertibly traumatic triggers such as sexual assault, child abuse, and cultural trauma, whilst those on the "anti" side often mention seemingly trifling things like name-calling, unusual phobias, or personal slights. It would be useful if everyone would consider the full multiplicity of experiences under the "trigger" umbrella.

In terms of what trigger warnings open up and close down,

they have the potential to increase the agency of people in a class, or reading a book, to decide whether and/or how they want to engage with it, potentially giving more power to people who have been most marginalized or traumatized. However, if taken too rigidly, trigger warnings could encourage us to divide the world in binary ways between the powerful people who should give trigger warnings, and the powerless victims who require them. This is another "us and them" scenario. The "powerless" can then become further disempowered by the assumption that they require looking after and can't take responsibility for their own experiences. The "powerful" can find that their own vulnerabilities are dismissed or ignored by others—and by themselves if they invest in this position.

An alternative approach involves not trying to determine which side you are on, or whether trigger warnings are a good or bad thing. Rather we could consider how we engage with the possibility of trigger warnings in ways which most enable their potential to open things up, whilst also being mindful of their potential to close things down, and also recognizing that, whatever we do, will not be perfect, and some closing down is probably inevitable—it is an ongoing process, not a once-and-for-all choice.

Thought experiment: Working through this structure

Having read through these two examples, try applying this structure to a debate that's familiar to you. Remember to ask yourself:

1. *Is this one thing or many? If many do we need to focus on just one aspect at a time?*
2. *What does it open up and what does it close down?*
3. *How might you creatively engage with it in this complexity?*

How did it feel to work through the debate in this way, rather than trying to decide what was right or wrong, good or bad?

So when we're drawn into polarizing about a certain issue, person, decision, or situation, perhaps we can ask ourselves in what ways it is multiple, complex, and changing, rather than slipping into fixing it as one unified, static, stable thing. That might involve remembering all of the different sides of a person in our life; or seeing the differences between people in a particular group or category as well as how they are similar to each other; or determining to consider a situation from as many different perspectives as we can.

When decision-making we could deliberately aim to consider options between and outside those we are currently imagining, perhaps writing down all of the options we can possibly think of. It might be helpful to recognize that we, ourselves, are multiple rather than singular, and giving a voice to all of our different perspectives on the matter—something we'll say more about in the final section of the chapter. We can consider what is lost and gained in each possible choice (including choosing not to choose), and what may open up and close down, rather than being tempted to see one way as all good and another as all bad.

Embracing uncertainty

Returning to Buddhism, a key approach here—to get away from binary thinking—is that of embracing uncertainty. Remember Martine Batchelor's example of holding the precious object from earlier? Buddhist teachers suggest that, rather than grasping tightly or hurling away, we can hold onto things gently and embrace the uncertainty that comes with this. Rather than leaping to conclusions and actions we can stay in the state of non-knowing for longer. This can be a painful place to be—because we struggle with uncertainty—and it can also be a relief from the intense struggle of all-or-nothing thinking, which can lead to more compassionate and wise decision-making. We might practice embracing uncertainty on easier matters in life to help us to do it on more loaded issues. This is what meditators do when they tune into the first tiny sensations, thoughts, and feelings which bubble up and try to notice whether they are labelling them as positive or negative, and what this leads to.

As Pema Chödrön puts it in her book *The Places That Scare You*:[5]

> Dwelling in the in-between state requires learning to contain the paradox of something's being both right and wrong, of someone's being strong and loving and also angry, uptight and stingy. In that painful moment where we don't live up to our own standards do we condemn ourselves or truly appreciate the paradox of being human? Can we forgive ourselves and stay in touch with our good and tender heart? When someone pushes our buttons do we set out to make the person wrong? Or do we repress our action with "I'm supposed to be loving. How could I hold this negative thought?" Our practice is to stay with the uneasiness and not solidify into a view... The crossroads is an important place in the training of a warrior. It's where our solid views begin to dissolve. There's no way to do this exactly right. That's why compassion, along with courage, is vital.

MJ explored the implications of this idea of embracing uncertainty throughout their book, *Rewriting the Rules*. They pointed out that, for any aspect of relationships, we're drawn to either cling tightly to existing rules from the culture around us, or to hurl them away and find alternative rules to cling to equally tightly. For example, we see this in the way some people grasp hold of the search for The One perfect partner, and others reject the whole possibility of love relationships due to cynicism or being burned too often. Many people cling tightly to the rules of monogamy, trying to evade any potential risk to their relationship with strict rules about how

---

5   Chödrön, P. (2013) *The Places That Scare You: A Guide to Fearlessness.* London: Element, p.189.

they and their partners can relate to others and who they can have relationships with. Other people shun and criticize monogamy, but come up with an equally rigid set of rules about how to do non-monogamous relationships (see Chapter 2).

Embracing uncertainty in these areas involves loosening our grip around relationship rules, and around other people, recognizing that there is no perfect set of guidelines or agreements that will keep us safe from pain, and that nobody can meet all of our needs all of the time. Once we're in that spacious place of uncertainty, again we have more capacity to be present to how things actually are, to explore creative possibilities for how we might deal with the situation in front of us, and to be flexible and embrace each other in our complexity and freedom.

Embracing uncertainty can also help us to cultivate understanding of ourselves and others. If we're not trying to polarize into us/them, good/bad, right/wrong, we might be better able to take the leap to empathize with where the other person is coming from, and to recognize that we—ourselves—are in multiple positions. An example of this relates to the binary of privilege/oppression which comes up in conversations where one person or group points out the oppressive or marginalizing behavior of another person or group. Like most people, we've found ourselves, countless times, on both sides of this divide, because—also like most people—we're marginalized in some ways and privileged in others (see Chapter 4).

How might it be, when we're on the privileged side of this dynamic, to remember what it's like to be on the oppressed side? We might remember just how much it took for us to point out to yet another privileged person how much their ignorant actions had hurt us, and see it as an act of trust on their part. We might consider how this kind of thing is probably a deeply wearing daily occurrence for this person, and understand why they may well be expressing anger and frustration. We might remember how most people probably respond defensively, however kindly they phrase what they're trying to say, and commit to not just being another of those people. On the flip side, when we're the one doing the calling out or calling in, can we remember how horrible it feels to have thought you were being a decent ally, only to realize you'd made a mistake and hurt people? Can we be mindful of how vulnerable it feels to fuck up and have that pointed out? Can we try to give people a bit of room to take it in, for example, or give them a second chance if their first reaction is defensive?

It's not easily done, and—of course—it shouldn't be on already marginalized people to do a bunch of emotional labour just in order to be heard; but embracing uncertainty invites us to make that uncomfortable leap to remember when we—ourselves—have been on the other sides of dynamics like privilege/oppression or consent violator/violated within a non-consensual culture where it's inevitable that we will sometimes abuse our privilege and act non-consensually towards others.

Let us be a little clearer; we're not arguing here for tending to the fragility that can accompany a certain level of privilege in dominant culture. We do believe it's essential for those of us with power and privilege to educate ourselves and to nurture our own resilience. Our own fragility cannot be yet another burden for those impacted by lack of power and privilege. However, we've also observed how within our own marginalized communities, we might—at times—target each other and assume that another person has more power and privilege than they actually do. This usually happens when people are triggered and in pain, and feel powerless in larger dominant culture.

Many of us are building community across historical, cultural, social, and intergenerational trauma with one another. It's a miracle we can even relate to each other in the midst of so much suffering! What we're advocating for is a culture of accountability and restorative practices, rather than a shunning, excluding, and cutting off, and a mindfulness towards multiple dimensions of power and privilege that might be at play in various situations.

We find that white social justice activism is particularly prone to more binary thinking of inside/outside and of excluding people, and we believe that this is part of white supremacy thinking, which favors ideas of perfectionism and purity. If we are to dismantle the very systems that oppress us, we cannot operate in the same way and use the same tools. This is where the work of activists of color, such as Mia Mingus with accountability pods, is particularly useful. We're being asked to imagine a different world, with systems of justice, healing, and restoration that might not be familiar to many of us (see the Further Resources at the end of this chapter).

Multiversal perspectives

We mentioned earlier in the book the idea of multiversality—that is the existence of multiple realities, stories, and possibilities. In some ways, this is the opposite of a universal view (only one way, one world, one story). In others, it could be argued that a multiversal view can contain the reality and possibility of the universal. The latter is simply one of the ways in which some people live. However it need not be the only way.

Tricksters across time and space seem often to be the beings that remind people about multiversality. Most Earth-based traditions—be they Indigenous ones, reconstructed older traditions, or neo-pagan ones—have stories about tricksters, or even deities who are tricksters; for example, Loki in Norse tradition, Anansi in both some West African and Caribbean traditions, Elegua in the Yoruba tradition, Eris in the Hellenic tradition, Kokopelli in Hopi tradition, Lugh in Celtic traditions, Wisakedjak in Cree and Algonquin traditions, and Laverna in Roman traditions.

Many tricksters—or deities with trickster moments—cross

boundaries, defy customs in some ways, and subvert or break the rules. Sometimes they're shapeshifters and gender benders. Often they are keepers of stories, and teachers. Usually they're associated with chaos in some way. Tricksters seem to exist to remind us to not get too settled into one way, or too rigid in our thinking and customs, even revered ones. Many tricksters are also connected to either some type of underworld, or spirit world, and to the crossroads. The crossroads are, in many ways, the liminal place where many roads meet, and from where many roads start. They can be a place of arrival as well as a place of beginning.

Multiversal perspectives allow us to remember curiosity, playfulness, and an openness to the unexpected, uncertainty, and change. In many ways change is the only constant in a multiversal view. Tricksters are essential because we might forget and get rigid in our ways, not letting things go when it's their time, and not letting the new come in. A multiversal view enables us to value the broad range of our humanity. For example, both the perspectives of children and young people—as well as the wisdom of elders—are needed when we function well as an intergenerational community, and adults can be the bridge between them. Nobody is more special than anyone else, yet we're all essential (thank you Donald L. Engstrom-Reese for your teachings on this; see Further Resources).

In order to live within a multiversal view, though, we need to learn to move away from a culture of scarcity—widely promoted by a settler colonial, capitalist, dominant culture—and towards a culture of abundance. We need to believe that you existing—in your full multi-hued, magnificent size and power—does not take away from me existing, in my own full multi-hued, magnificent size and power. This means also not subscribing to a culture of competition, which divides and pits the most marginalized against one another, given that this is how power-over cultures often thrive.

Multiversal perspectives then invite us to be in power with one another, rather than in power over one another. They are congruent with the idea of sovereignty over our own selves, thrive on relational and systemic views, can help us embrace inevitable change, and ask us to move away from binary thinking so that we can open up to the vast landscape of potentiality that non-binary thinking offers.

6.4 How to think non-binary

So can we just stop this habit of binary thinking? Not really. To misquote one of MJ's favorite films, *The Big Chill*, "I don't know anyone who could get through the day without two or three juicy polarizations". And probably we could replace "day" with "hour", or even "minute". Many of us have been binary thinking our whole lives, so it's not an easy thing to stop doing, and we need to go gently on ourselves, remembering that judging ourselves as good or bad on the basis of how much we are binary thinking is yet another binary. But perhaps, if we make space to pause several times each day and to notice how we are falling into binaries, we can create the possibility for other ways of engaging with our lives. And, if we do this, we may start to be able to bring such approaches to the big debates and issues which we find ourselves involved with.

Ongoing practices

Thinking non-binary, for many of us who were not brought up to do so, does indeed require daily practices of care. Sometime people talk about self-care but we'd like to invite you to think of interdependent care. Alex's friend, another MJ interestingly enough, was the first person to bring this idea to their attention. Talking about self-care locates the responsibility for change and caring practices within the individual, yet we live in a dominant culture in which systemic forces make it hard to care for ourselves.

Interdependent care then highlights the need for an ethics of care we can engage in—on a collective level—if we so choose.

What are some of the individual and collective practices that can help us practice non-binary thinking? We've already mentioned not treating the land, others, and ourselves as a commodity, for example. What does that look like? One of the ways in which we can practice this is attention and intention. Do we ask ourselves where our food and water come from? It doesn't need to be fancy or organic, what we're talking about here is feeling a sense of connection and interdependence in our day-to-day lives. When we find ourselves irritated by other people, can we ask ourselves what happens if we consider what might be going on for the other person? It's common for us to center ourselves when we're stressed or tired; our view then becomes narrow, and we might forget to consider how we're in the same web. Do we ask of ourselves more than we can actually give on a daily basis? Do we give ourselves the nourishment—physical, emotional, spiritual, and social—that we need?

We might have been brought up to put other people's needs above our own, and asking ourselves these questions might be challenging. We might not even know where to start! MJ has a useful zine about self-care (see Further Resources) and Alex, as always, reminds you to go back to the body. For example, the slow down page in this chapter was all about doing an activity that is kind for you. Were you able to do this? If you go back to the slow down page in Chapter 3, do you practice self-consent on a daily basis? Self-consent is maybe one of the most challenging forms of consent, as we keep pushing ourselves to do more than we can. What would happen if we practiced meeting our needs more, being a little kinder to ourselves? How might that change the way we also relate to others?

Practices that can support us in shifting our attention and

intention might include: journaling; eating slowly and mindfully at least once a day; the activities suggested in the slow down pages; meditation; taking a daily walk where we pay attention with all of our senses; practicing presence in one to two tasks per day, such as washing the dishes, taking a shower, or preparing a meal; dancing, singing, or creating something. Basically it's anything that enables us to slow down, reflect, and pay attention more closely to our experience, in the present moment, with curiosity, non-judgment and self-compassion, or activities that bring us in deeper relationship with ourselves.

Rituals are also important as we develop ongoing practices to move towards non-binary thinking. Do our days have some structure? If so how does that structure enable us to have more space and flexibility? We know that this seems paradoxical, but often structure can actually create more room for creativity as we're not spending so much of our energy in certain daily tasks, and in making a myriad of small decisions. Daily rituals also encourage us to think about what we would like our days to look like.

All of this requires patience, presence, and self-compassion. If we can be rooted in the idea that we're already worthy, without needing to do anything else, that we're enough, that we can simply be, these practices become easier. Of course this idea might seem unattainable. That too can become a practice: to tell ourselves that we're enough, that we can just be, that we can rest when we need to, and work when we need to, and listen to ourselves and meet our needs, that we're worthy and essential because we're alive. When we can do this, we practice challenging living in all/nothing thinking. It takes a long time for some of us to restore our nervous system so that we can have access to a much broader range of physical, emotional, social, and spiritual movement in our lives.

When we can learn to tolerate being with ourselves, everything changes. We can learn to trust ourselves, because we know that we will not continuously betray ourselves by crossing our own boundaries. We won't need to squeeze ourselves as much into either/or boxes because we'll be able to consider other possibilities, to be vulnerable, and to show up more authentically. A question that might be useful to explore can be "is there a third road here, another possibility?" In many ways, the main practice is to get to know ourselves more deeply and intimately. When we know and accept our history, our triggers, our experiences and how they impact the present, we might be better able to catch ourselves before we spiral into binary thinking. We can take a pause, a breath, and notice that a third road is usually there.

Thought experiment: Making an altar to yourself

In this thought experiment we ask you to do something that might seem a little weird, or maybe very familiar. If you're able, please go with it and notice what happens! We encourage you to find a space where you live to make an altar. If that's not possible, you can make a portable altar, or even a digital one. An altar is just a space—physical or virtual—where you can place objects to symbolize something. You can put whatever you want on this altar to yourself, although we strongly suggest including a mirror, if you're sighted. You may want to include pictures of yourself at different times in your life, or things that are important to you.

You may want to also include ancestors of blood, spirit, culture, or activism. Because we don't live in a binary world, there are many beings and things that make us who we are, including our ancestral connections. Be with this altar for a period of time. You may want to have it up for a week, a month, from new moon to new moon, or for a year, from birthday to birthday. Spend a little time with your altar every day. It can be just a few minutes. What do you appreciate on this altar? What is missing? What is present? You can add or change the altar as you want. What's it like to pay so much attention to yourself, and to spend intentional time with yourself, and to have yourself externalized in this way? As you spend time with yourself, you might want to notice which parts of yourself you might cling to, be proud of, and which you may want to hurl away, far from you, and separate from. Remember to always return to the breath, and to use as much self-compassion, curiosity and non-judgment as you're able. You may want to journal your reflections through writing or making art.

Non-binary thinking about our selves

Something that can help with interdependent care and self-compassion is thinking in more non-binary ways about ourselves. As we've touched on in previous chapters, dominant culture encourages us to think of ourselves as a singular, static, fixed self which can be compared against others, ideals, and norms, and judged and found wanting. This is the foundation of consumer capitalism—which sells us products on the basis of perceived "flaws" or "lacks", and it is the foundation of self-monitoring culture, whereby we all spend our time self-policing, which helpfully—to those in power—stops us from seeing the problems in wider culture and pressing for change.

We saw in the last chapter how many mental health struggles are related to this tendency to see ourselves as singular and static. For example, the harsh inner critic which many of us experience in the form of an internal—or external—voice is often all about berating us for our imperfections and holding us to impossible standards.

If we shift to a non-binary understanding of the self, we can loosen some of this grip of perfectionism, self-criticism, and self-monitoring. If we recognize that we're plural rather than singular, and in process rather than fixed, then it can be much easier to allow ourselves to care for ourselves, and to find compassion for ourselves.

Plural selves

What does it mean to say that we are plural selves, rather than a singular self which could be judged in binary ways against a perceived "other" (see Chapter 3)? Many schools of therapy have pointed out that most—if not all—people have sides to them which are so distinct as to be understood as separate selves. The inner critic and the inner child are well-known examples of such selves. An easy way to get a sense of this for yourself is to think about how you are in different relationships and situations in life, for example with a parent versus a friend versus a colleague, or when you're in a professional role, versus hanging out with close people, versus alone. Studies have shown that most of us bring very different sides of ourselves out in different relationships—or situations—even though we may experience ourselves as being "ourselves" or "authentic" in all these relationships and situations,

As we grow up we learn which selves are welcomed by those around us, and which are not, so we come to foreground some selves (e.g. those that get approval from others, or which are deemed appropriate to somebody of our gender, race, class, etc.) and disown others (e.g. those which are rejected by others or deemed inappropriate in our culture). It can be useful—as adults—to reclaim those disowned parts of ourselves and let them be part of our integrated whole being. For example, reclaiming the scared child can enable us to be more vulnerable, reclaiming angry warrior sides can help us to stand up for ourselves and keep our boundaries better. Improving communication between all the different selves is the key to being able to let all sides of ourselves have a voice, rather than keeping some foregrounded and others pushed down.

If we see ourselves—and everyone—as plural rather than singular it doesn't make any sense to judge ourselves in our entirety as certain kinds of people: good or bad, together or broken, useful or worthless, and so on. We may also find it easier to be more compassionate to sides of ourselves than we do when we see ourselves as singular. For example, can we cultivate a compassionate side of ourselves to care for the vulnerable creature who comes out when we're traumatized, or to give a break to the controlling side who wants to take over and protect us from harm? If these ideas resonate for you, there's more information about how to embrace our plural selves in the Further Resources at the end of this chapter.

Fluid selves

We've seen throughout this book how many aspects of us are better seen as a fluid process of becoming, rather than a fixed or static aspect of who we are. For example, the ways people express, identify, and experience their gender and sexuality often shift over time (see Chapters 1 and 2), as do many other intersecting aspects of who we are (see Chapter 3).

Again, recognizing that we are always—inevitably—a work in progress can be a relief which enables us to treat ourselves more kindly. However we are in this moment, that will inevitably change and change again, so we are never fixed forever in being this messed up, or this in pain, or this conflicted. We might think of ourselves like the river—always flowing on—rather than imagining that we are one cup of water taken out of that river at a particular moment in time.

Buddhist author Stephen Batchelor has this to say about regarding ourselves as unfolding stories, rather than fixed selves:

> So what are we but the story we keep repeating, editing, censoring, and embellishing in our heads? The self is not like the hero of a B-movie, who remains unaffected by the storms of passion and intrigue that swirl around him from the opening credits to the end. The self is more akin to the complex and ambiguous characters who emerge, develop, and suffer across the pages of a novel. There is nothing thinglike about

me at all. I am more like an unfolding narrative. As we become aware of all this, we can begin to assume greater responsibility for the course of our lives. Instead of clinging to habitual behavior and routines as a means to secure this sense of self, we realize the freedom to create who we are. Instead of being bewitched by impressions, we start to create them. Instead of taking ourselves so seriously, we discover the playful irony of a story that has never been told quite in this way before.[6]

Thought experiment: Your self beyond binaries

We came across a great way to consider our own relationship to binaries at a workshop run by our friends and Gestalt therapists Elizabeth Sune and Mihai Popeti. Here we've adapted it into an activity you can do by yourself, and also suggested a more embodied way you could do it in a group, if you have that opportunity.

If you can, on a big piece of paper write some binary opposites in the form of two poles like this:

o -- o
Work   Play
o -- o
Young   Old

You might want to include some of the binaries we've covered in this book around gender, sexuality, relationships, bodies, and emotions, for example. When you've got a few interesting binaries written down, work your way through them.

For each one in turn, take a moment to feel into where you are in relation to the binary, and then draw it on the page. It may be that

---

6   Batchelor, S. (1998) *Buddhism Without Beliefs*. London: Bloomsbury Publishing, p. 83.

you're at one end or the other of a spectrum between the two points, or in between, or in both extremes simultaneously—or in different contexts. You might locate yourself outside the binary entirely, or moving between different positions all the time. That binary might be completely irrelevant and you might want to draw a big cross through it. Anything goes here.

Once you've drawn something that feels right to you, if you want to you can also write down some words—or draw something—from that place. What does it feel like to be there in relation to that binary?

You could also draw something to depict where you've been in the past in relation to that binary, and where you imagine being in the future.

When you're done with that binary, move your body, shake it off, breathe and turn to the next one.

If you have the option of doing an activity like this in a group of friends, make two points in a room the binary poles. Then take turns to label those poles, and place your bodies between them to say where you are. You can move or shape your body to display how that feels, and say a few words from that place, before shaking off, moving around, and trying a new binary.

There's no right/wrong binary about what you do in your life to encourage non-binary thinking. Different things work for different people at different times. Here are a bunch of examples of how people do it. Whatever works for you is okay.

Multiple experiences: Practicing thinking non-binary

- "I find that formal meditation practice works for me. I read a bit from my favorite Buddhist author, then sit and try to notice my tendencies to get hooked into binary thinking: positive/negative, grasping/hurling away. Doing this with a group of people at the local Buddhist centre is super helpful to support my practice."

- "For me I have to write things down to make sense of them. I go to a cafe and get my journal out. I describe whatever it is that's bothering me at the moment till I've got it all out of my system, and then I reflect in my journal on how binary thinking might be keeping me stuck here."
- "I'm a geek so I'm all about tables and spreadsheets. When I have a decision to make I create a detailed table with all of the options on it, then I work through what each one would open up and close down for me, and what steps I'd have to take to do each one. I try to embrace uncertainty by keeping that document live through the whole process of making the decision, returning to it and changing the color codes which represent how drawn I am to each option."
- "I love conscious movement practices. It can be authentic movement, dance church, Nia, or just dancing in my PJs. I need to move my body to get in touch with how I feel. This also helps me shake off trauma responses and move away from those stuck places. When I move sometimes I cry, or laugh, or feel irritated. I love moving with other people who get it, who are there for the same reason I am, to feel more alive and move through the difficult places."
- "I'm a volunteer mediator. I love this role in my communities. I have learned so much through the training, such as how trauma shows up in conflict, and how to de-escalate heated situations. Mediating helps me cultivate compassion. I can be with people in their struggles with one another and notice how often those struggles are really with themselves. It helps me appreciate how messy we are as humans and how much work it can take to be in right relationship with one another."

- "I go to therapy every week. I have done so for years. Sometimes I think about stopping but there is something about having a space that is just for me that is so important. I can slow down, think about what's going on, what's working, and what could be different. I can get really stuck into extremes so it's helpful to have my therapist remind me that there are other options."
- "When I make time for ritual it's like I can breathe. I start from thinking, what is my intention, what do I need and want? Then I think about how to best explore that intention. Is it through sitting meditation, singing, a visualization, a journey, divination, a spell? Ritual gives me time outside of clock time. I can go within and also connect to the land and to spirit for guidance."

Further Resources

MJ's books, mentioned in this chapter, are:

- Barker, M-J. (2018) *Rewriting the Rules: An Anti-Self-Help Guide to Love, Sex and Relationships*. London: Routledge.
- Barker, M-J. (2018) *The Psychology of Sex*. London: Routledge and Psychology Press.

You can also find their blog posts and zines relating to these topic at:

- rewriting-the-rules.com/zines (Hell Yeah Self Care, Plural Selves and Social Mindfulness)
- rewriting-the-rules.com/self/trigger-warning-trigger-warnings-towards-a-different-approach
- rewriting-the-rules.com/conflict-break-up/privilege-oppression-conflict-compassion

Other useful books that deal with these topics, including those we've quoted here, are:

- Batchelor, M. (2001) *Meditation for Life*. London: Frances Lincoln. (stephenbatchelor.org)
- Batchelor, S. (1998) *Buddhism Without Beliefs*. London: Bloomsbury Publishing. (stephenbatchelor.org)
- Brooks, C.V. and Selver, C. (2007) *Reclaiming Vitality and Presence: Sensory Awareness as a Practice for Life*. North Atlantic Books.
- Brown, A.M. (2017) *Emergent Strategy: Shaping Change, Changing Worlds*. Chico, CA: AK Press.
- Chödrön, P. (2013) *The Places That Scare You: A Guide to Fearlessness*. London: Element. (pemachodronfoundation. org)
- Hagan, S. (1999) *Buddhism Plain and Simple*. London: Penguin.
- Okun, T. and Jones, K. (2000) *Dismantling Racism: A Workbook for Social Change Groups*. Atlanta, GA: dRworks.
- Phillips, W. (2015) *This is Why We Can't Have Nice Things: Mapping the Relationship Between Online Trolling and Mainstream Culture*. Cambridge, MA: MIT Press. (motherboard.vice.com/en_us/article/vb73zm/berkeley-doesnt-have-to-choose-between-social-justice-and-free-speech)
- Serano, J. (2013) *Excluded: Making Feminist and Queer Movements More Inclusive*. Berkeley, CA: Seal Press. (juliaserano.com)

And here are some further resources you might find useful:

- thedailybeast.com/how-both-sides-journalism-is-failing-transgender-people
- Chimamanda Ngozi's TED talk on "The danger of a single story": www.ted.com/talks/chimamanda_adichie_the_danger_of_a_single_story?utm_campaign=tedspread&utm_medium=referral&utm_source=tedcomshare, accessed on 21 November 2018.
- Donald L. Engstrom-Reese's website on queer spirit, queer heathenry and more: http://wearewalkinginbeauty.org
- On the characteristics of white supremacy culture: www.thc.texas.gov/public/upload/preserve/museums/files/White_Supremacy_Culture.pdf, accessed on 21 November 2018.
- Mia Mingus on accountability pods and pod mapping: https://batjc.wordpress.com/pods-and-pod-mapping-worksheet, accessed on 21 November 2018.
- A podcast about collective healing and social change: www.healingjustice.org
- Kristin Neff's website on self-compassion: http://self-compassion.org

Index